Defeating Evil

God's Plan
Before the Beginning of Time

Planet Earth - God's Testing Ground

Roger G. Gallop, Ph.D.

Copyright © 2018 by Red Butte Press, Inc.

Revised (2019, 2021)

All rights reserved. No portion of this book may be reproduced in any form without written permission of the publisher, except in the case of brief quotations in articles and reviews.

Roger G. Gallop, Ph.D.
Defeating Evil – God's Plan Before the Beginning of Time (Planet Earth - God's Testing Ground)
Library of Congress Control Number: 2018930391

ISBN-13:   978-0-9829975-2-9 (paperback)
ISBN-13:   978-0-9829975-3-6 (case laminate)

Red Butte Press, Inc.
P. O. Box 711
Ponte Vedra Beach, Florida 32004-0711

Scripture quotations marked NIV are taken from the *Holy Bible, New International Version*®, Copyright © 1973, 1978, 1984, 1985 by the International Bible Society. Used by permission of Zondervan Publishing House. Also, some Scripture quotations are taken from Bible Gateway, www.biblegateway.com.

Scripture quotations marked NAS are taken from the *New American Standard Bible*®, Copyright © 1960, 1962, 1963, 1968, 1971, 1972, 1973, 1975, 1977, 1995 by The Lockman Foundation. Used by permission. (www.Lockman.org)

Scripture quotations marked KJV are taken from the King James Version. Scripture quotations marked ESV are taken from English Standard Version.

Photographs and illustrations are by Roger G. Gallop or by authors who have granted permission; other photographs and illustrations have been released into the public domain by their author or U.S. Government agency, or the copyright has expired.

Graphics: Roger G. Gallop, or as shown on drawing.

Book Design/Layout: Roger G. Gallop

This book was written for educational and ministerial purposes.

Roger G. Gallop is also author of the books:
evolution – The Greatest Deception in Modern History (Scientific Evidence for Divine Creation)
World in Denial – Defiant Nature of Mankind (Prophetic Evidence for a Divine Creator)

Visit www.CreationScienceToday.com

contents

Preface vi
   In Reading This Book vi

Prologue vii
   Challenging Questions vii

Chapter 1: In the Beginning - God 1
   Who Is God? 1
   Causal Agent 2
   Where is God - Before and After Creation? 4

Chapter 2: Creation and Purpose of Angels 5
   Why Did God Create Angels? 7
   Choirs of Angels 8
   Roles of Archangels and Angels (Third Triad) 10

Chapter 3: Creation of Our Physical World (Days 1 - 6) 13
   The Original Supercontinent - Pangaea (4004 BC -- 2385 BC) 15
   Creation and Purpose of Mankind 16
   What is the Image of God? 19
   The Garden of Eden 20

Chapter 4: Origin of Evil 21
   The First Sinful Act 22
   Rebellion - Methodical, Deliberate, and Calculated 24
   Access to the Throne of God 26
   Final Eviction from Heaven 28

Chapter 5: Fall of Mankind 31
   Immediate Effects of the Fall 36
   Physical and Spiritual Death 38
   Individual Curses on Humanity 40

Chapter 6: Effects of Evil on Humanity 43
   Defiant Antediluvian (Pre-Flood) People (4004 BC - 2385 BC) 44
   Worldwide Flood - Restructuring of Pangaea (2385 BC) 46
   Continual Defiance of Mankind (2384 BC - Presetnt Day) 49

Chapter 7: The Problem with Free Will 53
- Free Will Makes Evil Possible 53
- Could Evil Have Been Avoided? 55
- Does God Have Limitations? 56

Chapter 8: Defeating Evil 57
- God's Provision for Sin 57
- Best Possible Solution 61
- Planet Earth - God's Testing Ground 63

Epilogue 65
- *Evil Still Exists in Our World* 65
- *Making the Right Choice* 67

Appendix A – Why Didn't God Make Us Like Angels? 70
Appendix B – Issues of Pain and Suffering 71
Appendix C – Is There an Eternal Hell? 77
Appendix D – Evidence for the Existence of God 83
- Scientific Evidence for Divine Creation 83
- The Bible's Prophetic Accuracy 85
- The Bible's Unity 87
- The Bible's Historical Accuracy 88
- The Bible's Preservation 89
- The Bible's Uniqueness 91
- The Moral Law 92
- Attempts to Destroy the Bible 93

Index 94

Bibliography 95

preface

> *"In the time of my favor I heard you, and in the day of salvation I helped you. I tell you, now is the time of God's favor, now is the day of salvation."* —2 Corinthians 6:2, NIV

This book is the second of a three book series on Creation (Genesis 1-2), the Fall of Man (Genesis 3), and the Defiant Nature of Mankind throughout history (Genesis 4 through Revelation). These books are:

- ***evolution – The Greatest Deception in Modern History (Scientific Evidence for Divine Creation)*** (2011, 2nd Ed. 2014, revised 2016, 2018, 2021) presents overwhelming scientific evidence for Divine Creation.

- ***World in Denial – Defiant Nature of Mankind (Prophetic Evidence for a Divine Creator)*** (2017, revised 2019, 2021) presents a historical perspective of the effects of evil (arrogance, immorality, depravity, violence, lawlessness, terrorism, greed, and idolatry) on humanity and prophetic evidence for a Divine Creator.

- ***Defeating Evil – God's Plan Before the Beginning of Time (Planet Earth - God's Testing Ground)*** (2018, revised 2019, 2021) is an overview of creation (including creation and purpose of angels, our physical world, and mankind); origin of evil; fall of mankind; the effects of evil on humanity; the problem with free will; and God's plan for defeating evil.

"...without faith it is impossible to please God, because anyone who comes to him must believe that he exists and that he rewards those who earnestly seek him" (Hebrews 11:6, NIV).

in reading this book

This book is presented in general chronological order beginning with creation and ending with the defeat of evil and the future of mankind.

Some explanations are found in 'text boxes' and Appendices A, B, C, and D provide additional explanations on more controversial subjects. Appendix D provides a summary of the evidence for the existence of God—scientific, prophetic, and historical.

Mankind denotes both man and woman. The letter 'c.' placed before dates of antiquity means 'about' and 'cf.' before Scripture means 'compare.' Some words such as cross and heaven may or may not be capitalized at the discretion of the author; the word hell is usually not capitalized unless it is in a quote or at the beginning of a sentence. The word Scripture is capitalized.

"Free will," "freedom," and "freedom of choice" have similar meanings, and these words or phrases are interchangeable. Some phrases and explanations about the problem of "free will," love, and evil are often repeated throughout the book for better understanding.

prologue

> *"For God so loved the world that he gave his one and only Son, that whoever believes in him shall not perish but have eternal life."* — John 3:16, NIV *"The reason the Son of God appeared was to destroy the devil's work."* — 1 John 3:8, NIV

This book describes the nature of God; creation and purpose of angels; creation of our physical world; the creation and purpose of mankind; the origin of good and evil, and the fall of mankind; the effects of evil (arrogance, immorality, depravity, lawlessness, violence, terrorism, greed, and idolatry) on humanity; the continuing problem of evil throughout history and in our world today; and God's solution in defeating evil.

The primary focus of the book is the nature and necessity of "free will" (freedom of choice); its relation with love and evil; the defiant nature of mankind; and life on earth as God's testing ground for mankind. The book answers most of the challenging questions concerning good and evil, and concludes by emphasizing the absolute necessity of making the right choice during life on earth.

challenging questions

Where did evil come from? Did God have a plan to defeat evil before laying the foundations of the world? Did the plan include preserving 'free will' and 'love'? And could a holy, righteous God create evil that permeates our world? If God is holy, righteous, and omnipotent, and if He did not create evil, where did it come from, and why did He allow evil to have its way?

Why is there so much arrogance, immorality, depravity, violence, lawlessness, terrorism, and greed in our world today and throughout all of history? If God is all good, holy, and righteous, why doesn't He immediately put an end to pain, suffering, misery, and tragedy? Could evil, pain, and suffering have been avoided?

Given the sum total of human misery and grief in the world, why did He create the world in the first place? Why does He not perform more miracles to avoid pain and suffering? And by what moral standard do we believe there is evil in the world? Is there any real evidence for the existence of a sovereign, holy, and righteous God?

Why didn't God create humans who would not sin? Scripture tells us that God is completely sovereign—so then, why does God permit evil? When evil first appeared, why didn't He just do away with evil 'then and there'? Again, He has the power to do so. Does He lack the compassion or the will?

Does God have limitations? If so, what are they? The answers may be surprising. So then, why did God create mankind and allow so much terrible pain, suffering, and heartache throughout history based on an idea (children of God; p. 18) that would eventually fail? When will God bring an end to evil and the world's misery? Is earth a testing ground for mankind?

Is there an eternal hell? Why did God create people He knew would go to hell? Why will some people suffer (forever) in hell? Will there be a good end to life on earth?

Chapter 1

In the Beginning - God

> *"In the beginning was the Word, and the Word was with God, and the Word was God. He was in the beginning with God. All things came into being through Him; and apart from Him nothing came into being..."* — John 1:1–3, NAS

Who Is God?

The proper name for God is *Yahweh*, or *"the Lord"*. He is the Creator of the heavens and the earth and all that exists (Jeremiah 10:12-16, 51:15-19; Isaiah 40:28, NIV). The Bible teaches there is only one true God and He is completely loving, just, and holy (Isaiah 6:1-3, 57:15; Psalm 99:5; Habakkuk 1:13; Psalm 5:5-6; and Leviticus 20:26).

> *"...the name of the Lord, the Eternal God"* (Genesis 21:33, NIV); *"His ways are eternal"* (Habakkuk 1:12, 3:6, NIV); *"...everlasting to everlasting"* (1 Chronicles 16:36, 29:10; Nehemiah 9:5; Psalm 103:17, 106:48, NIV); *"Your throne, O God, will last for ever and ever"* (Hebrews 1:8, NIV); *"I am the Alpha and the Omega, the First and the Last, the Beginning and the End"* (Revelation 1:8, 21:6, 22:13, NIV); *"And they will reign for ever and ever"* (Revelation 22:13, NIV); and *"As God told Moses, 'I AM WHO I AM'"* (Exodus 3:14, NIV).

God is the great Creator—the power *inside and outside the universe*. He created time and space, the stars and constellations, the earth, and all life including mankind, *"God saw all that He had made, and **it was very good...**"* (Genesis 1:31, NIV). [Bold added] "No one survives without the good that God provides: love, peace, hope, beauty, health, and relationships (to name a few)." (Bickel & Jantz, p. 19)

People lest not forget the Lord is omnipresent, omnipotent, and omniscient (Romans 8:29; Ephesians 1:4-5; 1 Corinthians 2:7), and *"the Lord is a warrior"* (Exodus 15:3, NIV)—*"He does whatever pleases Him"* (Psalms 115:3, 135:6; Job 23:13; Daniel 4:35, NIV), and *"He is to be feared"* (1 Chronicles 16:25; Psalm 96:4; Isaiah 8:13; Job 25:15-16, NIV).

Fearing God helps us overcome our own sinful nature. If a man is known to be God-fearing, we are likely to "trust that person more" and if people fear God they are "more likely to keep their word and treat others with kindness." (Reardon, p. 1) Our primary sin throughout history is that *"there is no fear of God before their [our] eyes"* (Romans 3:18, NIV).

Omnipresent is ever-present, everywhere, infinite. **Omnipotent** is all-powerful, almighty, supreme; unlimited in power. **Omniscient** is all-knowing; having complete or unlimited knowledge, awareness, or understanding; perceiving all things.

> *"He is to be feared"* (1 Chronicles 16:25; Psalm 96:4; Isaiah 8:13; Job 25:15-16; Matthew 10:28, NIV). "Scripture is full of commands to fear God, and it is also full of commands not to be afraid...[and] once our sins are confessed, He tells us in Romans 8:15 that we can come to Him saying, "Abba! Father!" (meaning "Papa" or "Daddy"). We are welcome to go boldly before His throne with the access permitted only to the King's children. We still fear Him but in a way that does not diminish our love for Him or His for us." (Alcorn, 2017, p. 11)

Most importantly, *"God is love"* (1 John 4:8, 4:16, NIV). The word "love" in this verse is translated 'agape love' found only in humans and God (Romans 5:8)—an unconditional, self-sacrificing love. (See Prologue, Good and Evil in the book by Roger Gallop, *World in Denial - Defiant Nature of Mankind*.) He created us to have fellowship with Him, and He sacrificed His Son to restore that fellowship, *"For God so loved the world that he gave his one and only Son, that whoever believes in him shall not perish but have eternal life"* (John 3:16, NIV).

Causal Agent

How did the universe progress from nothing without a causal agent (that is, a Divine Creator), thus denying the First and Second Laws of Thermodynamics (as described in chapter 2 of the book by Roger Gallop, *evolution - The Greatest Deception in Modern History (Scientific Evidence for Divine Creation)*, and the Law of Causality (cause and effect; every effect has a cause), and how did life and human consciousness come into existence? Regarding the Law of Causality, "the following reasoning stands up to scrutiny:

- Everything which has a beginning has a cause
- The universe has a beginning
- Therefore the universe has a cause."
(Catchpoole, p. 164)

As authors explain in *The Creation Answers Book*, "It is important to stress the words 'which has a beginning.' The universe requires a cause because it had a beginning... God, unlike the universe, had no beginning, so does not need a cause. In addition, Einstein's general relativity [theory], which has much experimental support, shows that time is linked to matter and space. So, time itself would have begun along with matter and space at the beginning of the universe. Since God, by definition, is the creator of the whole universe, He is the creator of time. Therefore, He is not limited by the time dimension He created, so He has no beginning in time. Therefore, He does not have, or need to have, a cause." (Catchpoole, p. 18)

> **God is outside and inside the universe, and He created matter and energy; time is linked to matter and energy; so therefore He is not limited by time.**

God is the Creator—the power within and outside the universe. The Bible teaches there is only one true God who is completely loving, just, and holy. *"I am the Alpha and the Omega, the First and the Last, the Beginning and the End"* (Revelation 22:13, NIV). As God told Moses, *"I AM WHO I AM"* (Exodus 3:14, NIV).

As C.S. Lewis explains, "If there was a controlling power **outside the universe**, it could not show itself to us as one of the facts inside the universe—no more than the architect of a house could actually be a wall or staircase or fireplace in that house. The only way in which we could expect it to show itself would be inside ourselves as an influence or a command trying to get us to behave in a certain way. And that is just what we do find inside ourselves. Surely this ought to arouse our suspicions?" [Bold and Italics added] (Lewis, C.S., p. 24)

Barred Spiral galaxy

Spiral galaxy

Milky Way Galaxy

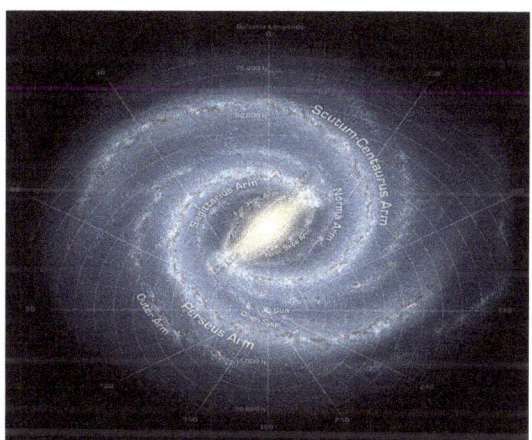

Milky Way Galaxy with two major stellar arms wrapping from the ends of a central bar of stars

> Who created God? God is an eternal being that has always existed—nobody created Him. God is the Self-Existent One—the great "*I AM*" of the Bible.
>
> "*In the beginning God created the heavens and the earth. And the earth was formless and void, and darkness was over the surface of the deep; and the Spirit of God was moving over the surface of the waters*" (Genesis 1:1-2, NAS). This was an instantaneous act of creation including all the light at the same time. The phrase *"heavens and the earth"* refers to the entire universe including space and time.

Where Is God Before and After Creation?

When God created the universe He was outside the universe (perhaps as theorized in quantum physics as a parallel universe) in what is described in the Bible as a third heaven.

> If space is curved as predicted by Einstein (now we are in the realm of quantum physics, space-time, parallel universes, and wormholes), then light could travel 10 to 20 billion light years in just a few thousand years—or one might say that the other side of the universe is just a stone's throw away.
> (Gallop, 2016, chapter 9)

A "third heaven" is mentioned in 2 Corinthians 12:1-4 wherein Paul called it "Paradise" in verse 4. Revelation 4:2 reveals that God's throne is in heaven—obviously, not the first or second, which are subject to time and space, but rather, as Paul wrote in 2 Corinthians, the third heaven refers to the location of the throne of God. (See Deuteronomy 10:14; Hebrews 9:24; Revelation 11:19.) (Gallop, 2016, chapter 9)

> Paul states in 2 Corinthians 12:1-4 (NIV), ¹"*I must go on boasting. Although there is nothing to be gained, I will go on to visions and revelations from the Lord. ²I know a man in Christ who fourteen years ago was caught up to the* **third heaven.** *Whether it was in the body or out of the body I do not know—God knows. ³And I know that this man—whether in the body or apart from the body I do not know, but God knows—⁴was caught up to paradise. He heard inexpressible things, things that man is not permitted to tell.*"
> [Bold added]

Artist's conception of a super massive black hole tearing apart a star

Stars in nearby galaxy: Genesis Creation Reveals that God is Eternal

The evidence of a third heaven implies a first and second heaven. The first heaven is the atmosphere of the earth (Psalm 104:12), and the second heaven comprises the stars of heaven and their constellations (Isaiah 13:10).

God, the architect and creator of the universe, was the controlling force outside the universe. Where is God after creation? He is omnipresent, omnipotent, and omniscient (Romans 8:29; Ephesians 1:4-5; 1 Corinthians 2:7), and His throne is in the third heaven (outside our known universe).

Chapter 2

Creation and Purpose of Angels

> *"God spoke to Job saying: 'Where were you when I laid the foundation of the earth? Tell me, if you have an understanding, when the morning stars sang together and all the sons of God [angels] shouted for joy?'"* — Job 38:4, 7, NAS

We do not know exactly when and where angels were created—the Bible is not specific about this subject. Angels sang and shouted for joy following creation (Job 38:4, 7) *which suggests they existed before creation*, but it is clear they did not exist from all eternity (Nehemiah 9:6; Psalm 148:2, 5). How long ago before creation of the earth no one knows.

> *"God spoke to Job saying: Where were you when I laid the foundation of the earth? Tell me, if you have an understanding...when the **morning stars** sang together, and all the **sons of God** shouted for joy?"* (Job 38:4, 7, NAS) [Bold added]

The *"morning stars"* and "*sons of God*" (Job 38:4, 7) are angels. Supporting Scripture concerning *"the sons of God"* is: *"One day the sons of God came to present themselves before the Lord, and Satan came among them"* (Job 1:6). (See chapter 4, section Access to the Throne of God.)

Angels are immortal celestial spirits (Hebrew 1:14; Luke 20:35-36) who were created to represent God and to defend His interests (Psalm 148:5-60); they are to praise the Lord because He created them and made them secure in the created universe. Angels have no physical body although their spiritual forms have human features (e.g., feet, faces, and voices; Isaiah 6:1-2, and presumably legs, arms, and hair).

Angels are mentioned over 100 times in the Old Testament and over 160 times in the New; therefore, we are able to make inferences and draw some conclusions.

Angels are very intelligent (Matthew 8:29; 2 Corinthians 11:3; 1 Peter 1:12); show emotion (Luke 2:13; James 2:19; Revelation 12:17); each has an individual personality and will (Luke 8:28-31; 2 Timothy 2:26; Jude 6); and they are always obedient to God's commandments.

Angels are spiritual beings without matter and no body (Hebrews 1:14; Luke 24:39), therefore, they never age or change; they do not marry (Matthew 22:30), so they do not have children; they cannot suffer physical pain or death (Luke 20:34-36)—but in reference to fallen angels, we know that angels can suffer spiritual death (separation from God) (Luke 8:21; Matthew 24:41; Revelation 20:14), and can suffer in some other way (Matthew 8:29; Luke 8:28).

Humans, on the other hand, are limited by their physical bodies (physical brain) and effects of the fall (see chapter 5, section Immediate Effects of the Fall, regarding the first and second laws of thermodynamics and genetic burden) and do not understand things as completely as angels—consequently, they do not fully grasp the consequences of their choices.

They can take the appearance of an ordinary man or appear as a dazzling radiant figure. (In Matthew 28:2-4, NIV, *"His appearance was like lightning, and his clothes were white as snow."*) Angels do not marry or produce offspring (Matthew 22:30), and they are not a race like humans—rather, they are a fellowship of spiritual beings with special categories of authority and dignity (titles and ranks). See section, Choirs of Angels.

Angels were bestowed with great intellect, understanding, wisdom, power, and holiness—and they were granted "free will." (Why "free will"? Without "free will" there is no love. See chapters 4-7 for more information.) Also, the Bible does not state that angels were created in the image of God as it does for mankind (man and woman) in Genesis 1:26-27.

The intellect and wisdom of angels allow them to grasp God's commands instantly, clearly, and completely, but they are not omniscient (2 Samuel 14:20; Matthew 24:36). Although in spirit form angels are able to move from one place to another quickly (Daniel 9:21), they can only be in one place at a time (they are not omnipresent), and they are much stronger than humans (but they are not omnipotent; Psalm 103:20; 2 Peter 2:11).

The number of angels is unknown but Scripture indicates that they are countless, *"Then I looked up and heard the voice of many angels, numbering thousands upon thousands, and ten thousand times ten thousand"* [an indefinitely large number; 100 million] (Revelation 5:11, NIV). Revelation 9:16, NIV, states 200,000 million; see Matthew 25:53; Daniel 7:10; Hebrews 12:22.

Human intelligence in today's world **has been degraded** since the fall of mankind as a result of the 2nd Law of Thermodynamics and mutations; see chapter 5, Fall of Mankind, specifically pp. 36-37 of this book.

Also refer to the book by Roger Gallop, *evolution – The Greatest Deception in Modern History (Scientific Evidence for Divine Creation)*, specifically chapters 2 and 3, Physical Scientific Evidence for Creation and Biological Scientific Evidence for Creation; see sections Universal Decay and Conservation of Matter/Energy, Entropy and Heat Death, De-Evolution, Law of Biogenesis - Origin of Life, Natural Selection and Extinction, Mutations – Deformities and Disease, and Human Intelligence, etc. Angels have no such limitations.

As stated in the above cited book, "...many people are under the misconception that our generation is the healthiest and most intelligent that has ever lived. **This is not the case.** Modern technology of this generation does not mean that we are the most intelligent or the healthiest—in fact, quite the contrary. We have accumulated technological knowledge while, during the same period, our brains and bodies have endured 6,000 years of mutations and degeneration." (Gallop, p. 37)

Refer to the book, *All the Angels in the Bible,* by Herbert Lockyer, Jr. This is a rewrite of the original work by his father, *The Mystery and Ministry of Angels*. This book can be purchased on Amazon.

Why Did God Create Angels?

Why did God create angels? The Bible tells us that angels were created to love God and to be God's messenger or agent to carry out His plans for creation.

But more importantly, angels are continually returning to the presence of God. Why? Because of their love and happiness by being close to God the Creator and their

> The word "angel" means "messenger" or "agent." The Bible says, *"Praise the Lord, you his angels, you mighty ones who do his bidding, who obey his word"* (Psalm 103:20, NIV).

fellowship with God. When humans get a glimpse of angels, they [angels] are often radiating the beauty of God's splendor. They are still "white" from being in His presence, much like Moses was "radiant" after being in the presence of God on Mount Sinai when he received the Ten Commandments. When Moses came down from Mount Sinai he was not aware that his face was glowing.

"When Moses came down from Mount Sinai with the two tablets of the covenant law in his hands, he was not aware that his face was radiant because he had spoken with the LORD" (Exodus 34:29, NIV).

"In the midst of the living beings there was something that looked like burning coals of fire, like torches darting back and forth among the living beings. The fire was bright, and lightning was flashing from the fire. And the living beings ran to and fro like bolts of lightning" (Ezekiel 1:13-1, NIV).

"It shone with the glory of God, and its brilliance was like that of a very precious jewel, like a jasper, clear as crystal" (Revelation 21:11, NIV).

Source: Unknown
Public Domain

An angel comforting Jesus before his arrest in the Garden of Gethsemane.
Artist: Carl Bloch (1834 -1890)

Choirs of Angels

All Angels are not equal in majesty, splendor, or dignity. There are three triads and three choirs of angels in each triad, or a total of nine choirs or classes mentioned in the Holy Scripture; the highest are called Seraphim, and the lowest are called Angels. The Archangels are one class higher than the angelic hosts of regular Angels. (ChurchPOP, p. 1-3)

First Triad: The first three choirs of angels attend to God directly.

The first choir are the mighty **Seraphim** (plural for Seraph), meaning "the burning or fiery ones," who have the most intense love for God and praise God singing *"Holy, Holy, Holy is the Lord Almighty; the whole earth is full of his glory"* (Isaiah 6:1-7, NIV). These angels are very large with six wings; two wings cover their faces because even Seraphim cannot look directly upon God; another set of wings cover their feet because they are on holy ground; and two are for flying.

The second choir are the mighty **Cherubim** (plural for Cherub), which means "fullness of wisdom"—these angels meditate on God's wisdom and understanding. They are double-winged and are guardians of God's glory and assigned to protect special places on earth. They symbolize God's glory, power, and mobility. In the New Testament, they are alluded to as celestial attendants in the Apocalypse (Exodus 25:18-21; Ezekiel 10:14; Revelation 4-6).

The third choir are **Thrones**, which represent the faithfulness of the love of God. These angels are known for their brilliant minds—they are full of peace and humility and contemplate God's will. They meet directly with God to discuss His plans and purpose for everyone and everything, and meditate on God's awesome power and judgment (Ezekiel 10:17; Colossians 1:16; Daniel 7:9).

The Assumption of the Virgin by Francesco Botticini at the National Gallery London shows three hierarchies and nine orders of angels, each with different characteristics.

God created Lucifer who was an anointed cherub (Ezekiel 28:13-17; Isaiah 14:12-14). Lucifer's name means "Light Bearer," a name which indicates great beauty; the "Bright One" or "the son of the morning." He was referred to as the 'covering angel.' Just as Cherubim covered the mercy seat of the Ark of the Covenant, Lucifer was created by God to be the angel of worship and to dwell eternally in the throne room of heaven, in the presence of God (Ezekiel 28:14).

According to Ezekiel 28:13 (NIV), we learn that Lucifer was a magnificent angelic being: *"You were in Eden, the garden of God; every precious stone adorned you: ruby, topaz and emerald, chrysolite, onyx and jasper, sapphire, turquoise and beryl. Your settings and mountings were made of gold; on the day you were created they were prepared."* Adorned with gold and precious stones, his intellect and wisdom far exceeded that of other angelic beings.

Second Triad: The second three choirs fulfill God's plan for the universe.

The fourth choir are **Dominions** which have authority over the lower choirs and humanity. They are angels of leadership; they regulate the duties of angels and make known the commands of God. They take direction from the higher choirs (first triad) and oversee the universe (Ephesians 1:21; Colossians 1:16).

The fifth choir are **Virtues** which sustain the movement of the universe including planets, seasons, and weather. They are in charge of miracles and provide courage and perseverance for mankind (Ephesians 1:21).

The sixth choir are **Powers** which assist in governing the natural order. They are warrior angels given authority to defend the universe and the world, and fight the war against demonic (fallen) beings who attempt to attack mankind (Ephesians 3:10, 6:12).

Third Triad: The third three choirs interact with and serve humanity.

The seventh choir are **Principalities** which are assigned to care for and guard nations, states, and communities, and they are associated with transitions of leadership power within nations and states (Ephesians 3:10; 1:21).

The eighth choir are the **Archangels** which are assigned to carry out God's most important plans for mankind. They deliver God's most important messages to man, and Scripture identifies two by name — Gabriel (Luke 1:26) and Michael (Daniel 12:1). Gabriel's name means, "God is Mighty"; Michael's name means, "One who is like God."

The ninth choir are the **Angels** which are closest to the material world and humanity. This choir is where we find most of the personal **Guardian Angels** (Luke 22:43; Matthew 18:10; Hebrews 13:2).

Archangel Michael
Artist: Guido Reni (1575 - 1642)

Angels are mentioned in the following Scriptures:

- Seraphim - Isaiah 6:1-7; Psalm 24:1, 72:19; Exodus 3:6; Job 4:18, 15:15; I Kings 19:13.
- Cherubim - Ezekiel 1:5-18, 10:12; Genesis 3:24.
- Archangels - Jude 9 (Michael, Gabriel).
- Angels - over 300 times in Bible.
- Sons of God - Genesis 6:1-2; Job 38:7; Daniel 3:25-28; Psalm 29:1, 89:6-7, 103:20, 104.4; Isaiah 13:3; Joel 3:11; Daniel 9:21; Hebrews 1:7.
- Watchers/Keepers - Daniel 4:13-17; Isaiah 62:6.
- Holy Ones - Zechariah 14:5; Matthew 25:31; Isaiah 6:1-3; Daniel 8:13.
- Princes - Daniel 10:13, 20-21, 12:1; John 12:31, 14:30, 16:11; Ephesians 2:2.
- Thrones - Colossians 1:16; Revelation 4:2-11.
- Dominions - Colossians 1:16.
- Principalities - Colossians 1:16, 2:10; Ephesians 1:21, 6:12.

Roles of Archangels and Angels
(Third Triad)

As described in the previous section, angels have various levels of authority or dignity (choirs of angels). The last three choirs comprise Principalities, Archangels, and Angels. These choirs have different roles in heaven and on earth which include:

> Overseeing the transition of government power (Ephesians 3:10; 1:21); messengers to men (Acts 7:52-53, 8:26, 10:1-8; Matthew 1, 2); attend to physical needs (Genesis 21:17-20; 1 Kings 19:6; Matthew 4:11); protect and deliver (Daniel 3; Acts 5 and 12); strengthen and encourage through perseverance (Matthew 4:11; Acts 5:19-20, 27:23-25); answer prayers (Daniel 9:20-24, 10:10-12; Acts 12:1-17); care for believers at the time of death (Luke 16:22); executioners (2 Kings 19:20-34); minister to God's people (Hebrews 1:14); and serve as Guardian Angels (Daniel 12:1; Psalms 34:7, 91:11; Luke 22:43; Matthew 18:10; Hebrews 1:14, 13:2).

God utilizes His angels to deliver messages and execute His judgments (see chapters 4 and 5 in the book, *World in Denial – Defiant Nature of Mankind*), and they rarely draw attention to themselves as they carry out assignments. Angels protect and encourage God's people; they accompany the lonely and forsaken, and have interceded in human military battles throughout history. There are cases where these heavenly beings strike terror in the hearts of God's enemies (1 Samuel 14:20; Exodus 23:27; 2 Kings 19:35, 6:8-23; Deuteronomy 7:23, 28:7). When delivering messages angels began their words saying, *"Do not be afraid,"* or *"Do not fear."* Most of the time, "God's angels operate undercover and don't draw attention to themselves as they carry out the assignment given them by God." (All About God, p. 1)

Are angels sent to punish men? Yes, this is sometimes the case. Angels led Joshua into battle in the land of Canaan; an Angel killed 185,000 men in the army of a wicked king who had blasphemed God (2 Kings 19:35); an Angel slew the first-born in the families of the Egyptians who had persecuted God's people (Exodus 11, 12).

Regarding the role of ministering to God's people, angels whom the Bible calls *"Ministering Spirits"* have many roles and tasks to assist the Christian. *"Are not all angels ministering spirits sent to serve those who will inherit salvation?"* (Hebrews 1:14) They minister to God's people and deliver messages of support and reassurance.

Some angels "are created to perform specific tasks such as Guardian Angels of countries, territories and individuals"—for example, countries such as Israel and the U.S.; cities such as Jerusalem; and individuals (heads of state to the least among us). The Archangel Michael is the guardian of Israel (Daniel 12:1). Psalm 91:11 says, *"He will command His angels about you, to guard you in all your ways."* In time of temptation these angels can provide direction, courage, and strength, and present our good works and prayers before God (although God already knows and has already heard our prayers). Guardian Angels are able to help and protect us as children and as adults. (Russell, p. 1)

Guardian Angels are assigned to children at the time of their birth and are able to minister to them throughout their lifetime (Matthew 18:10; Psalms 34:7, 91:11; Hebrews 1:14). Guardian Angels pray for us, protect and guide us, and offer our prayers, good works and sometimes intercede on our behalf with prayer requests to God.

The Bible says, *"For he will command his angels concerning you to guard you in all your ways"* (Psalm 91:11). This includes not only physical danger, but moral and spiritual danger as well.

Personal Experience: When I was eight years old on a canoe trip, I saw a radiant figure sitting on a tree limb high up along the river embankment of a remote, heavily wooded area. I immediately knew who he was although I knew nothing about such things and we never spoke.

I didn't know what a Guardian Angel was until that moment. Several years later while I was on a bicycle crossing a busy highway, I was physically pulled back (although I was alone) and kept from being run over by a speeding car that missed me by just a few inches. I never told my parents what happened.

Later I felt his presence as he watched over me and those around me while in the jungles and mountains of Vietnam and Laos when my life was often in peril, and years later during dark, very sad periods of my life. During such times prayers were answered—but there were other long periods when I felt terrible heartache but never felt the angel's presence.

Three angels visiting Abraham
Artist: Ludovico Carracci (1555 - 1619)

Chapter 3

Creation of Our Physical World
(Days 1 - 6)

> *"In the beginning God created the heavens and the earth. And the earth was formless and void, and darkness was over the surface of the deep; and the Spirit of God was moving over the surface of the waters."* — Genesis 1:1-2, NAS
> The phrase *"heavens and the earth"* refers to the entire universe including space and time.

On the first day (Genesis 1:1-5) there was an instantaneous act of creation including all the light at the same time.

"In the beginning God created the heavens and the earth. And the earth was formless and void, and darkness was over the surface of the deep; and the Spirit of God was moving over the surface of the waters" (Genesis 1:1-2, NAS). The phrase "heavens and the earth" refers to the entire universe including space and time.

"Then God said, 'Let there be light'; and there was light. And God saw that the light was good; and God separated the light from the darkness. And God called the light day, and the darkness He called night. And there was evening and there was morning, one day" (Genesis 1:3-5, NAS).

> In verse 3, God made light—but it didn't say God made the sun. The sun is not needed for day and night—just light and a rotating earth. Thus, if we have light from one direction and a revolving earth, there can be day and night. On the first day, light was created to provide day and night until God made the sun on day 4.

God is the Creator—the power within and outside the universe. The Bible teaches there is only one true God, and He is completely loving, just, and holy.
"I am the Alpha and the Omega, the First and the Last, the Beginning and the End" (Revelation 22:13, NIV). As God told Moses, *"I AM WHO I AM"* (Exodus 3:14, NIV).

The expansion or *"stretching out"* of the universe is supported by Biblical Scripture. In Isaiah 42:5 (NIV), it states *"This is what God the Lord says, he who created the heavens and **stretched them out.**"* [Bold added] Jeremiah 10:12 (NIV) states, *"But God made the earth by his power; he founded the world by his wisdom and **stretched out the heavens** by his understanding."* [Bold added] And Zechariah also emphasized the "stretching out" of the heavens in the end-of-days prophecy— prophecy we are experiencing today.

> *"This is the word of the Lord concerning Israel. The Lord, who **stretches out the heavens**, who lays the foundation of the earth, and who forms the spirit of man within him declares: I am going to make Jerusalem a cup that sends all the surrounding peoples reeling. Judah will be besieged as well as Jerusalem. On that day,*

> This is an effortless stretching out of one's hand like the stretching out of a "paper daisy chain." The matter-energy did not come from within the universe but flowed into the universe (from outside). Other related Biblical Scriptures include Job 9:8; Psalm 104:2; Isaiah 40:22, 40:28, 44:24, 45:12, 45:18, 48:13, 51:13; and Jeremiah 51:15.

when all the nations of the earth are gathered against her, I will make Jerusalem an immovable rock for all the nations. All who try to move it will injure themselves" (Zechariah 12:1-3, NIV). [Bold added]

As confirmed by the Anthropic Principle, the universe is not a random or chance event. According to Isaiah 45:18 (NIV), *"For this is what the Lord says—he who created the heavens, he is God; he who fashioned and made the earth, he founded it; he did not create it to be empty, but* **formed it to be inhabited**—*he says, I am the Lord, and there is no other."* [Bold added]

> **Anthropic Principle** - the universe was designed in a very precise manner to support life. For more information, see chapter 2, The Anthropic Principle, in the book by Roger Gallop, *evolution - The Greatest Deception in Modern History (Scientific Evidence for Divine Creation)*.

On the second day (Genesis 1:6-8) the atmosphere was formed. The atmosphere as we know it today (that is, the troposphere, stratosphere, mesosphere, thermosphere, ionosphere, and exosphere) would not have existed during initial creation. However, Genesis 2:4-6 implies periodic rainfall, a normal hydrologic cycle, and moderate seasonal variations during the pre-flood period. (See next section.)

On the third day (Genesis 1:9-10) land was made to appear above the surface of the waters. This was a great orogeny as landmasses (rocks and the primitive earth, or the primeval supercontinent, Pangaea) were uplifted above the waters. (The next section describes the primeval supercontinent, Pangaea.) This was the first of two worldwide tectonic upheavals—the other was the great orogeny associated with Noah's flood described in chapter 6. On the same day (Genesis 1:11-13) God made vegetation.

On the fourth day (Genesis 1:14-19) God established the sun, moon, and stars with respect to the earth, and on the fifth day (Genesis 1:20-23) God created all sea creatures and birds after their kind. On the sixth day God created all land animals and mankind—this is described in the section, Creation and Purpose of Mankind.

The Original
Supercontinent - Pangaea
(4004 BC - 2385 BC)

From a biblical and young earth perspective, the original ancient continent was created by God as a single landmass about 6,000 years ago: *"Let the waters below the heavens be gathered into one place, and let the dry land appear"* (Genesis 1:9, NAS). By the end of the 1,600-year antediluvian period (4004 BC – 2385 BC) just before the worldwide flood (see chapters 4 and 10, *evolution – The Greatest Deception in Modern History (Scientific Evidence for Divine Creation)*, it is believed the population was more than 250 million people, and society was sophisticated, perhaps comparable to the early Egyptian culture.

Pangaea is the primeval supercontinent composed of all the major landmasses.

Today's continents and countries are shown to give the reader an idea how the ancient landmass, Pangaea, relates to the current world. Obviously, these modern-day countries did not exist in 4004 BC - 2385 BC.

The approximate location of Eden in the ancient world can be reasonably approximated. See chapter 6, section Worldwide Flood - Restructuring of Pangaea (2385 BC), p. 46.

Climatic and topographic conditions were much different from our current world. Although the supercontinent had mountains, rivers, and seas, its topography was much less prominent than we know today—the oceans weren't so deep and the mountains weren't so high (i.e., high hills and plateaus). There were other significant differences. The climate was similar to today's temperate regions with moderate seasonal variations (Genesis 1:14, 8:22). A milder environment can be verified by fossils of tropical plants found in today's polar regions.
(Dillow and Whitcomb)

Creation and Purpose of Mankind

On the sixth day (Genesis 1:24-25) God created all land animals after their kind, and then on the same day, God created man (male and female) after His own image and gave them dominion over all living things.

> "Then God said, 'Let us make man in our image, **according to our likeness**; and let them rule over the fish of the sea and over the birds of the sky and over the cattle and over all the earth, and over every creeping thing that creeps on the earth.' **And God created man in His own image, in the image of God He created him; male and female He created them**. And God blessed them; and God said to them, 'Be fruitful and multiply, and fill the earth, and subdue it; and rule over the fish of the sea and over the birds of the sky, and over every living thing that moves on the earth.' Then God said, 'Behold, I have given you every plant yielding seed that is on the surface of all the earth, and every tree which has fruit yielding seed; it shall be food for you; and to every beast of the earth and to every bird of the sky and to every thing that moves on the earth which has life, I have given every green plant for food'; and it was so. And God saw all that He had made, and behold, **it was very good**. And there was evening and there was morning, the sixth day" (Genesis 1:26-31, NAS). [Bold added]

At this point in time when the heavens and the earth were created, we are told the *angels sang and shouted for joy* following creation which suggests that angels existed before creation of the universe (Job 38:4, 7), but it is clear they did not exist from all eternity (Nehemiah 9:6; Psalm 148:2, 5), and they were likely not created in heaven (see chapter 4 for more information). How long ago before creation of the earth no one knows—but we might speculate angels were created before creation of the universe and mankind.

Creation of Mankind

Genesis 1 describes the role of Adam and Eve in relation to the entire universe. *"So God created man in His own image, in the image of God He created him; male and female He created them"* (Genesis 1:27, NIV). [Bold added] *"Then God said, I give you every seed-bearing plant on the face of the whole earth and every tree that has fruit with seed in it. They will be yours for food"* (Genesis 1:29, NIV) (*"whole earth"* meaning Pangaea, a vast landmass).

Genesis 2 narrows the focus to the Garden of Eden (see map of Pangaea on previous page), a region in what is now modern day Iraq. Before creating Adam,

> We know that God created angels before He created man, but there is no evidence in Scripture that God created angels in His image. No angels manifest the "likeness of God"—but rather, this is a unique honor that God gave to man. Man was made in the likeness of God for His glory.

God planted various trees in Eden that were all *"pleasing to the eye and good for food"* (Genesis 2:9). *"The Lord God formed the man from the dust of the ground and breathed into his nostrils the breath of life* [soul and spirit -

consciousness] *and the man became a living being"* (Genesis 2:7, NIV). Then God created the woman, Eve, from the rib of Adam (Genesis 2:21-22).

> When God breathed into Adam (and into Eve) the breath of life, mankind was given some of God's attributes *"in the image of God He created him"*— not necessarily physical likeness but rather spiritual likeness.
>
> God reveals that He created human beings in His own image and likeness (Genesis 1:26-27)— language that **indicates offspring or children of God** (Genesis 5:1-3).

The Lord created the Garden specifically for Adam, the first human, whom God had formed. In Genesis 2:8-9, NIV, we read: *"Now the LORD God had planted a garden in the east, in Eden, and there He put the man He had formed. And the LORD God made all kinds of trees grow out of the ground— trees that were pleasing to the eye and good for food."*

God gave man (male and female) dominion over the entire world (Genesis 1:26-28, 5:1-2). God created a perfect world (Genesis 1:31)—no death, struggle, violence, cruelty, or bloodshed—and everything was "upheld" by God (Colossians 1:17 and Hebrews 1:3). There was no degradation, decay, or death. Adam and Eve were created good (sinless) and bestowed with great intelligence; they had fellowship with their creator, God the Father; and they were to rule over the earth. And *"God blessed them and said to them, 'Be fruitful and increase in number; fill the earth and subdue it'"* (Genesis 1:28, NIV). Every plant and tree was provided for their food.

The Garden of Eden by Thomas Cole (1801 - 1848)

Purpose of Mankind

Why did God create mankind? Scripture clearly states that God created man for His glory [beauty, splendor, and wonder] (Isaiah 43:7); also, that **mankind** (man and woman;6 see Genesis 1:27, 5:1) **was created to be children of God.** God desires that mankind love Him because *"God is love"* and He is the creator and father of all human beings. The purpose of mankind is stated at the beginning of Scripture. God reveals that He created human beings in His own image and likeness (Genesis 1:26-27)—language that **indicates offspring or children of God** (Genesis 5:1-3; Romans 8:14-17).

> ²⁶*"Then God said, **'Let us make man in our image, according to our likeness;** and let them rule over the fish of the sea and over the birds of the sky and over the cattle and over all the earth, and over every creeping thing that creeps on the earth.'"*
>
> ²⁷*"And God created man in His own image, **in the image of God He created him; male and female He created them**"* (Genesis 1:26-27, NAS). [Bold added]
>
> ¹*"In the day when God created man, He made him in the likeness of God. ²He created them male and female, and He blessed them and named them Man [mankind] in the day when they were created."*
>
> ³*"When Adam had lived one hundred and thirty years, he became the father of a son in his own likeness, according to his image, and named him Seth"* (Genesis 5:1-3, NAS).

In obedience to God the Father, humans will be allowed to share God's divine existence forever as children of God and rule over creation with Him (Genesis 1:28).

> **The reason for our existence is to become a member of the family of God**—His family, in His image and bearing His name, to eventually appear in His glory (see 1 John 3:2). **Every 'human being' living today has the "free will" opportunity to become a member of that divine, eternal family!**
>
> Paul speaks of this in the following Scripture. *"The Spirit itself beareth witness with our spirit, that we are the **children of God: and if children, then heirs—heirs of God, and joint-heirs with Christ....**"* (Romans 8:16-17, KJV). [Bold added]

"God blessed them and said to them, 'Be fruitful and increase in number; fill the earth and subdue it. Rule over the fish of the sea and the birds of the air and over every living creature that moves on the ground'" (Genesis 1:28, NIV).

*"Now if we are children, then **we are heirs of God and co-heirs with Christ,** if indeed we share in His sufferings in order that we may also share in His glory"* (Romans 8:17, NIV). [Bold added]

And most remarkably, just as human children are the same kind as their parents, so will we be the same kind of beings as God the Father and Jesus Christ—divine beings. It is beyond our capability to truly understand or comprehend what it means to be divine—to be like God the Father and our Lord Jesus Christ. We were given some of God's unique spiritual traits. **Our purpose is to be part of God's family** (Ephesians 3:14-15). Presently, God's family consists of three divine beings: God the Father, Jesus Christ, and the Holy Spirit, but God intends to increase this divine family into hundreds of millions or billions.

What is the Image of God?

There is no explicit definition in Scripture of what exactly comprises "the image of God"—so we can only speculate or perceive from scripture.

The image of God is love, morality (moral law), righteousness, justice (fairness), grace, and mercy. (Ham, S., Wallace, J.W.) In Genesis 2 it states that mankind (man and woman) were uniquely created in the (spiritual) image of God. What makes humans unique from other animals is not just physical but intangible differences such as creativity, culture, abstract reasoning, moral judgments, and a spiritual connection to our Creator. (Deem)

Other attributes associated only with humans is the ability to make "moral judgments"—even apes are unable to make moral judgments about the behavior of other animals. No other species of animal, including apes, displays a sense of morality (or conscience)—that is, remorse, shame, and guilt. (See chapter 3, section Uniqueness of Human Beings in the book by Roger Gallop, *evolution – The Greatest Deception in Modern History (Scientific Evidence for Divine Creation.)*

What other traits make humans unique from other creatures? Humans are able to appreciate the beauty of nature. In abstract reasoning, humans are able to invoke unobservable images to explain why things happen whereas other creatures operate in the observable world of tangible things—that is, the world that can be seen.

Another difference between humans and other animals is the "spiritual connection" between humans and the Creator. Both Adam and Eve had a personal, direct relationship with God, and such an association is not described for any other living creature. It is the presence of a "spirit" that separates humans from animals. As stated in Genesis 2:7 (NIV), *"...the Lord God...breathed into his nostrils the breath of life [spirit], and the man became a living being."*

There are three forms of life that God has created in this universe: (Deem)

   1. Body only. Examples are reptiles, amphibians, fish, invertebrates and other lower forms of life.
   2. Body and Soul. Examples are birds and mammals.
   3. Body, Soul, and Spirit. Examples are humans and angels.

The soul is the eternal part of a living being, separate from the body, and it is essential to consciousness and personality—the soul may be synonymous with the mind, will, and emotion. (Consciousness is awareness; personality is a psychological portrait of a person; mind is intellect that includes thought, perception, memory, emotion, and imagination; will [including "free will"; see pp. 56, 61-63] is the ability to make choices free from limitations; and emotion is associated with mood, temperament, personality, disposition or habit, and motivation.) Only birds and mammals display these characteristics, which is why humans can form close relationships with birds and mammals.

The spirit is that part of humans that is able to love and experience God directly—it allows humans (and angels) to have a relationship with the Creator. The soul and spirit are connected but separate (Hebrews 4:12)—the soul is who we are, but the spirit connects us with God. In Romans 8:16-17 (NAS), *"The Spirit Himself bears witness with our spirit that **we are children of God**. Now if we are children of God, **we are heirs—heirs of God and co-heirs with Christ**, if indeed we share in his sufferings in order that we may also share in his glory."* [Bold added] (See 1 John 3:2.)

Although sin has terribly altered the "image of God" in man (Romans 3:23; Isaiah 59:1-4), it is only through the atonement and resurrection of the Savior, Jesus Christ, that mankind can be forgiven and transformed to the image of God (Romans 8:28-30; Ephesians 4:24; Colossians 3:5-10; 2 Corinthians 3:18).

The Garden of Eden

The Bible does not provide much detail about the Garden of Eden except that Eden means "pleasure." Originally God created earth for man's pleasure and sustenance. The Garden of Eden offered both beauty, food, and nourishment being home to every tree *"that were pleasing to the eye and good for food"* and a source of fresh water from the river to drink. As for man, God *"put him in the Garden of Eden to work it* [cultivate] *and take care of it"* (Genesis 2:9, 15, NIV).

The Garden of Eden by Jacob Savery (1601)

> [10]*"A river watering the garden flowed from Eden; from there it was separated into four headwaters.* [11]*The name of the first is the **Pishon**; it winds through the entire land of Havilah, where there is gold.* [12]*(The gold of that land is good; aromatic resin and onyx are also there.)* [13]*The name of the second river is the **Gihon**; it winds through the entire land of Cush.* [14]*The name of the third river is the **Tigris**; it runs along the east side of Asshur* [ancient city of Assyria]. *And the fourth river is the **Euphrates**"* (Genesis 2:10-14, NIV). [Bold added]

Genesis 2:10-14 makes it clear that the Garden of Eden was located where four rivers derive from one headwater or source. Some believe the Garden was an outlet for freshwater springs because we read, *"a river flowed out of Eden to water the garden; and from there it divided and became four rivers"* (Genesis 2:10, NAS). These riverheads were the Tigris, Euphrates, Pishon, and Gihon, according to Scripture.

The physiography and topography of the original Eden were eventually destroyed and overlain by millions of tons of sediment deposition during a worldwide flood as described in chapter 6 (Worldwide Flood -- Restructuring of Pangaea) and more thoroughly described in the book by Roger Gallop, *evolution - The Greatest Deception in Modern History (Scientific Evidence for Divine Creation)* (chapters 4 and 10).

Chapter 4

Origin of Evil

> *"How you have fallen from heaven, morning star, son of the dawn! You have been cast down to the earth, you who once laid low the nations!* [13] *You said in your heart, "I will ascend to the heavens; I will raise my throne above the stars of God; I will sit enthroned on the mount of assembly, on the utmost heights of Mount Zaphon.* [14] *I will ascend above the tops of the clouds; I will make myself like the Most High."* — Isaiah 14:12-14, NIV

Would a holy, righteous God create evil that infiltrates our world— an evil that spreads "like an unstoppable deadly virus." Some people might logically draw the following conclusion: 1) God created all things (Genesis 1), 2) evil is real and permeates our present world and has been documented throughout history, so 3) people might assume that God created evil. Some people use this logic as a reason to reject or turn away from the Creator God of the Holy Bible or to blame God for their misfortune. But is this inference 'that God created evil' a valid assumption? (Arnaud, p. 27)

We know from Scripture that God created all things and He created only good things (Genesis 1:1, 3-4, 9-31; John 1:3; Colossians 1:16-17; 1 Timothy 4:4; Hebrews 1:3; Revelation 4:11, ESV). We also know from Scripture that God of the Bible is absolutely perfect—completely loving, just, and holy (Isaiah 6:1-3; Psalm 99:5; Habakkuk 1:13; Psalm 5:5-6; Isaiah 57:15). If God's creation is absolutely good; that is, God created only good things, then where did evil come from?

We are fully aware that evil is flourishing throughout the world (arrogance, immorality, violence, depravity, lawlessness, terrorism, and greed). It permeates everything and affects everyone—it is epidemic throughout our society, and it is vividly portrayed on a

---

Evil — is sin or iniquity; or choosing not to obey God. The consequences of evil are pain, suffering, decay (deterioration), disease, and death.

- **Moral evil** is disobeying God—it is breaking the moral law (see Appendix D, last section, The Moral Law), or any one of the Ten Commandments, or a departure from goodness.

- **Physical evil** is immorality, lawlessness, violence, depravity, corruption, and persecution with its ensuing pain, suffering, decay, disease, and death. Physical evil is the result of moral evil (disobeying God; the Moral Law) in some way. See Appendix B.

When we think of evil we think of tyrants and dictators, mass murderers, and people twisted into psychotic monsters who commit crimes against the innocent. Massacre of children and their families, and beheadings in the Middle East and worldwide by Islamic extremists is the face of evil today. In today's world, evil is in the hearts of all men (Genesis 6:5; Jeremiah 7:19).

> The Bible asserts that God created all things. *"In the beginning God created the heavens and the earth"* (Genesis 1:1, NIV); *"All things were made through Him..."* (John 1:3, NKJV); *"For by him all things were created: things in heaven and on earth, visible and invisible"* (Colossians 1:16, NIV); the saints in heaven sing to God, *"You created all things, and by your will they existed and were created"* (Revelation 4:11, ESV).

continual basis on national and world news, and documented throughout the c. 6,000 year history of mankind. See book by Roger Gallop, *World in Denial – Defiant Nature of Mankind (Prophetic Evidence for a Divine Creator).*

> Paul said, *"For everything God created is good"* (1 Timothy 4:4, NIV). Through God *"all things hold together"* and He continuously restored everything in the beginning (Colossians 1:17 and Hebrews 1:3).

So if everything God made was good (including the Seraphim and Cherubim, archangels and all the millions of other angels; and mankind: Adam and Eve), then how exactly did evil find its way into the world? <u>How did absolute good become the source of absolute evil—and, if God is holy and righteous and omnipotent and omniscient, why did He allow evil</u>?

The First Sinful Act

We know that God created nine choirs of angels and a beautiful Cherub called Lucifer (Ezekiel 28:14-15) sometime before the creation of the universe. Genesis 1:31 tells us everything was **very good** at the end of creation week, and the angels shouted for joy (Job 38:4, 7; see chapter 3, section Creation and Purpose of Mankind), **so we can rightly assume that Lucifer had not fallen**—he had not yet committed the first sinful act.

When God created angels, they were bestowed with great intellect, wisdom, and various levels of power and authority, and holiness, and the love of God. Angels were also granted "free will" (Luke 2:13-14; 2 Timothy 2:26; 2 Corinthians 11:3, 14)— <u>because without "free will" there is no love;</u> otherwise, angels would have been created as robots unable to love and enjoy friendship or companionship (2 Corinthians 11:3, 14).

Their intellect and wisdom allowed angels to understand situations instantly, clearly, and completely. As an angel, it would have been almost impossible to turn away from God. The love of God by angels is too great—God is their Creator, and the life of angels is magnificent and fulfilling. Turning away from God would have been equivalent to humans voluntarily jumping into a fiery furnace—humans would never consider such an idea, and angels would never consider turning away from God. Logically, one would never consider turning against someone you truly love.

So how could sin arise under such perfect conditions? What caused a perfect Cherub such as Lucifer to sin? **The answer goes back to "free will" which is the power to choose for or against God.** And again, why did God create angels with free will? Because there is **no love without freedom (free will)—otherwise angels would have been created as machines unable** to love and enjoy friendship. <u>Logically, if freedom (free will) is good, then evil is possible</u>.

> We can speculate that angels were not created in heaven, otherwise sin would have been impossible.

What caused Lucifer to sin? Ironically, Lucifer was the cause (source or maker) of his own sin by committing the first sinful act of **Pride** (1 Timothy 3:6). And how did this happen? With the power of "free will," **<u>Lucifer's love of God shifted to himself</u>. Lucifer began to adore himself; he exalted and rejoiced in his own beauty and desired to be as God in splendor, power, and authority.** Lucifer sinned when he made himself, rather than God the Father and Creator, the object of his attention and adoration (love). Psychologists today call this **narcissism, or self-love.**

> Lucifer was not tempted by God—God does not tempt anyone (James 1:13). **Lucifer sinned by his own choice, or by his own "free will."**

Sadly, most people in the world today are guilty of this very sin to one degree or another, and **most do not realize this sense of superiority, vanity, self-importance or self-love is the sin of <u>Pride</u>**—one of the seven deadly sins (pride, greed, lust, envy, gluttony, wrath, and sloth). **Pride is a high opinion of one's importance, and it pervades most of mankind.** People today look upon pride as a virtue—an attitude that reflects the depravity of mankind.

In today's world, it is not surprising that pride is viewed by most as a good thing—as a virtue—for example, people today are encouraged to take pride in their work, in themselves, and in all that they do. <u>Pride leads to conceit, arrogance, haughtiness, and superiority which is the very nature and essence of mankind today</u>.

> Lucifer, a Cherub angel, was highest reigning angel among the rebel angels. Only Seraphim rank higher than Cherubim.
>
> *"Your heart was lifted up [in pride] because of your beauty; you corrupted your wisdom by reason of your splendor"* (Ezekiel 28:13-17, NASB).
>
> Isaiah 14:12-14 (NIV) further describes Satan's sin:
>
> *[12]How you have fallen from heaven, morning star, son of the dawn! You have been cast down to the earth, you who once laid low the nations!*
> *[13]You said in your heart, "I will ascend to the heavens; I will raise my throne above the stars of God; I will sit enthroned on the mount of assembly, on the utmost heights of Mount Zaphon.*
> *[14]I will ascend above the tops of the clouds; I will make myself like the Most High."*

Rebellion
Methodical, Deliberate, and Calculated

Lucifer turned away from God because he was overcome with self-adulation and lust for power, and was convinced that God had no solution to the problem of "free will" which makes evil possible. Lucifer had a plan to rule the earth and possibly the first and second heavens. He was determined to establish his own authority and sovereignty (dominion) that mankind might worship him (honor and praise).

When Lucifer sinned he chose to disobey God, and he clearly understood the consequences of his decision. Lucifer's motivation was to alienate man from God (Genesis 3) and God from man (Zechariah 3:1; Revelation 12:9-10)—<u>alienation he believed could not be reconciled</u>. Lucifer's decision was methodical, deliberate, and calculated.

Lucifer knew that **once evil was loosed upon the world through the sin of Adam and his descendants, evil would permeate everything and everyone (and, in fact, it has to this very day). He believed there was no viable solution available to God—there was no plan that included the defeat of evil without the destruction of "free will and love," and that all mankind would be separated (alienated) from the Creator. Consequently, Lucifer believed he would rule the earth, mankind, and the first and second heavens.**

A third heaven is mentioned by the apostle Paul in 2 Corinthians 12:1-4. The evidence of a third heaven implies a first and second heaven. The first heaven is the atmosphere of the earth (Psalm 104:12), and the second heaven comprises the stars of heaven and their constellations (Isaiah 13:10). The third heaven, not subject to space and time, refers to the location of the throne of God.

There is no love without freedom but freedom also makes evil possible.
Once evil is loosed upon the world, it permeates society "like an unstoppable deadly virus" and even the very innocent suffer. See Romans 6:23 and James 1:15. (Arnaud, p. 27)

God foreknew the problem with "free will," love, and evil. <u>**The problem can be briefly described as follows**</u>: **Without "free will" there is no love but "free will" also makes evil (sin) possible, and because God's nature is completely opposed to evil (sin) (Isaiah 6; Habakkuk 1:13), Lucifer believed that God had an unsolvable problem: eliminating evil without destroying free will, love, and mankind who is immersed in sin (immorality, depravity, violence, lawlessness, terrorism, greed, and idolatry).** See pp. 61-63.

According to Scripture, a considerable following of rebellious angels (about a third of the lower ranked angels; Revelation 12:4) chose to follow Lucifer who coveted God's power and authority (Ezekiel 28:14-15; Isaiah 14:12-14; Revelation 12:4, 7-8; 1 Timothy 3:6). And like Lucifer, these other angels had no excuse.

Once angels turned away from God (Revelation 12:7-8), there was no turning back—and there was no redemption. Once they "choose" disobedience, it is equivalent to a human's final decision about their belief in God of the Bible while on earth and at the time of death (Hebrews 9:27). The Bible never calls upon fallen angels to repent as it does people (Acts 17:30). Fallen angels fell by the act of pride (1 Timothy 3:6), and they cannot be restored or saved.

When Lucifer sinned he and his following of rebellious angels were cast down from heaven to earth (Isaiah 14:12-15; Ezekiel 28:12-19; Revelation 12:7-8; Jude 6). Lucifer and his angels *"lost their place in heaven,"* and he became known as "Satan," a name which literally means "Adversary" as well as "Devil," which also means "Accuser of the brethren."

Lucifer was brought down to the earth because of evil in his heart—<u>**a sin of pride, or self-love or self-admiration, and a lust for power like many in the world today**</u>; for example, most of our politicians and world leaders. Sometime thereafter (perhaps within a few hundred years) was the temptation and fall of mankind (Genesis 3) as described in chapter 5 (Fall of Mankind).

Before the beginning of time God had a plan to preserve free will and love, and defeat evil. (See chapter 8 for more information.) Lucifer did not foresee (nor did he anticipate) the Son of God dying on the cross for man's sins. *"He [God] disarmed the rulers and authorities [Lucifer and the rebellious angelic host] and put them to open shame, by triumphing over them"* (Colossians 2:15, ESV).

As Randy Alcorn explains in his book, *If God is Good*, "From the beginning, God planned that his Son [Jesus Christ] should deal the death blow to Satan, evil, and suffering, to reverse the Curse [see chapter 5], *redeem a fallen humanity, and repair a broken world."* (Alcorn, p. 51)

"The reason the Son of God appeared was to destroy the devil's work" (1 John 3:8, NIV). In our present state, man is sinful and separated from God; Jesus Christ is God's only provision for man's sin.

Once angels sin, they are condemned forever with no prospect of redemption. *"God did not spare angels when they sinned, but sent them to hell..."* (2 Peter 2:4, NIV). Christ did not die for angels: *"...For surely it is not the angels that he helps, but he helps the offspring of Abraham"* (Hebrews 2:14-16, ESV).

Why would Satan embark on such a rebellion against a Sovereign God if he knew his plan would be futile? Because Satan was convinced that once evil was loosed upon the world through the sin of Adam and his descendants, evil would permeate everything and everyone, and <u>there was no viable solution for God—there was no plan that included the defeat of evil without the destruction of freedom, love, and mankind</u>, and all created beings (fallen angels and all human beings) would be separated from the Creator.

God the Creator (who is omniscient, omnipotent, and omnipresent) knew of the potential problem of "free will" from the beginning and had a plan before laying the foundation of the world—a plan that would allow **"free will" where love is preserved and sin is defeated.** More on this plan in chapters 7 and 8.

Why didn't God create angels who He knew in advance would not sin? The answer is, "there is no love without freedom"—God would simply be creating robots or androids.

Then why didn't God create angels with free will and annihilate those he knew in advance would rebel? This, again, would be subverting the very nature of free will—creatures free to either choose for or against God. God cannot demand that you either love me or I'll annihilate you—this of course is absurd. Mankind (created beings) must be free to choose, either for God or against God—and freedom makes evil possible.

Access to the Throne of God

Many people assume that a holy God is unable to tolerate sin, but this is a misconception. Psalm 139 describes God as being everywhere and fills heaven and earth, and therefore He is around and through everything (omnipresent), and fully aware of sin since the fall of Lucifer. Throughout Scripture we know that God can reveal Himself or can be "in the presence of" sin or sinners in some fashion—for example, meetings with Moses and others on Mount Sinai (Exodus 19:16-17) and the meeting between God and Lucifer as described in the Book of Job (see following Scripture, Job 1:6-12).

It is not a question of God being unable to tolerate sin—but rather, sin is completely (wholly) opposed or contrary to God's nature (Isaiah 6; Habakkuk 1:13)—sin creates a barrier between man and God. Sin separates us from God but through the sacrifice of Jesus Christ on the cross our relationship with God is restored—our sin is forgiven and no longer creates a barrier (Romans 3:23-24). Certainly, God can tolerate sin but **His nature requires sin or evil to be eventually purged (eliminated) from creation.**

One might ask the question: How is it that Satan was able to go before God as described in the book of Job (c. 2200 BC)? (Job 1:6-12, NIV)

> *⁶"One day the angels came to present themselves before the LORD, and Satan also came with them. ⁷The LORD said to Satan, 'Where have you come from?" Satan answered the LORD, "From roaming throughout the earth, going back and forth on it."'*
>
> *⁸"Then the LORD said to Satan, 'Have you considered my servant Job? There is no one on earth like him; he is blameless and upright, a man who fears God and shuns evil.'"*
>
> *⁹"Does Job fear God for nothing? Satan replied. ¹⁰ 'Have you not put a hedge around him and his household and everything he has? You have blessed the work of his hands, so that his flocks and herds are spread throughout the land. ¹¹But now stretch out your hand and strike everything he has, and he will surely curse you to your face.'"*
>
> *¹²"The LORD said to Satan, 'Very well, then, everything he has is in your power, but on the man himself do not lay a finger'"* (Job 1:6-12, NIV).

We assume the meeting place in the book of Job (Job 1:6-12) was the throne room of God in the third heaven. Following the first sinful act of Pride, Satan did not have open access to God's presence but, rather, <u>Satan was summoned by God</u>. The time before God's throne was temporary, and by God's power, the purity of Heaven (assuming the third heaven) was not infected (tainted) by the brief, God-ordained presence of a sinful being (Satan).

"When we say, 'God cannot allow sin into heaven'...but it is possible for God to command a sinful being to stand (temporarily) in His presence in order to commission him (Isaiah in Isaiah 6), to obtain an account from him (Job 1:6-12), or to judge him (Revelation 20:11-15) without compromising His holiness." (Got Questions, Does God still have access to Heaven?)

Job lived in Uz (in the East, in the vicinity of Edom) around 2200 BC before Abraham (born c. 2166 BC) and before Moses (born c. 1526 BC).

In the Book of Job, it is clear that God permits Satan (a fallen angel) briefly into His presence so He can demonstrate the faithfulness of his servant, Job. It is likely that Satan remained confident, arrogant, and prideful in God's presence—in a sense, Satan elevated himself. Although Satan could not foresee the future, from the start he (Satan) was convinced that the problem with "free will," love, and evil, and the defiant, sinful nature of mankind could not be resolved by God—and ultimately, he could win the battles and the war, and rule earth and the first and second heavens.

At the time of creation of our physical world (c. 4004 BC; see chapter 3), **Satan was not aware of God's plan for the redemption of mankind.** He certainly did not anticipate the Son of God, Jesus Christ, dying on the cross as a sacrificial lamb for the sins of mankind—the possibility would have been completely unfathomable (inconceivable) to Satan.

Scripture does not reveal when Satan first knew of God's plan of redemption for mankind. At or before the time of Moses (who wrote the first five books of the Bible [the Pentateuch or Torah including Genesis 3:15:] dated c. 1446 BC to c. 1406 BC, or about 750 years after the meeting with God about Job), **Satan likely began to realize or anticipate God's plan for the redemption of mankind**—so he initiated further steps to seize control: eradicate the Hebrew race; deter and kill the Messiah, Jesus Christ; and destroy the church.

> Genesis 3:15 is the first prediction relating to the Savior of the world, called 'the seed of the woman.' See chapter 5, section Individual Curses on Humanity and p. 222, item #18 regarding Genesis 3:15 in the book by Roger Gallop, *World in Denial – Defiant Nature of Mankind (Prophetic Evidence for a Divine Creator).*

In addition to the Scripture in Genesis 3:15 (see text box), there may be an inference in 1 Peter 1:12, NIV, *"...when they spoke of the things that have now been told you by those who have preached the gospel to you by the Holy Spirit sent from heaven. **Even angels long to look into these things.**"* [Bold added] It appears that the angels wanted to look into the gospel plan but were unable, and **if the angels did not know, it is certain that Satan did not know as well.**

For more information, see Appendix C, Satan's Attempts to Seize Total Control, and epilogue, #18, in the book *World in Denial – Defiant Nature of Mankind.*

> God foreknew the problem with "free will," love, and evil. **The problem can be briefly described as follows:** Without "free will" there is no love but "free will" also makes evil possible, and because God's nature is completely opposed to evil (sin), God had to eliminate evil without destroying free will, love, and mankind who is immersed in sin (immorality, depravity, violence, lawlessness, terrorism, pride, greed, and idolatry).
>
> Sin separates man and God—sin brings decay and degradation, and ensuing pain, suffering, and disease. The Bible states, *"For the wages of sin is death, but the gift of God is eternal life in Christ Jesus our Lord"* (Romans 6:23, NIV).

Final Eviction from Heaven

Revelation 12:7-12 concerns the casting out of Satan <u>two times</u>: <u>Verses 12:7-8, and Jude 6, are the original casting out of heaven</u> when Lucifer and his angels *"lost their place in heaven."* <u>Verses 9-12 are the final defeat and exclusion (eviction) from heaven following the birth, life, death, and resurrection of the Savior, Jesus Christ</u>. See note 12:9 in the NIV Study Bible.

1. <u>They lost their place in heaven</u> (following Satan's sin of self-love and pride):

*⁷"And there was war in heaven. Michael and his angels fought against the dragon, and the dragon and his angels fought back. ⁸But he was not strong enough, and **they lost their place in heaven**"* Revelation 12:7-8, NIV.

*"And the **angels did not keep their positions of authority** but abandoned their own home..."* Jude 6, NIV.

2. <u>Final defeat and eviction of Lucifer and the rebel angels</u> (following Jesus Christ on the cross as a sacrificial lamb for all mankind):

*⁹"The great dragon was **hurled down**— that ancient serpent called the devil, or Satan, who leads the whole world astray. **He was hurled to the earth, and his angels with him**. ¹⁰Then I heard a loud voice in heaven say: "Now have come the salvation and the power and the kingdom of our God, and the authority of his Christ. For the accuser of our brothers, **who accuses them before our God day and night, has been hurled down**.*

¹¹"They overcame him by the blood of the Lamb and by the word of their testimony; they did not love their lives so much as to shrink from death. ¹²Therefore rejoice, you heavens and you who dwell in them! But woe to the earth and the sea, because the devil has gone down to you! He is filled with fury, because he knows that his time is short" (Revelation 12:9-12, NIV). [Bold added]

As an angelic being of authority (a Cherub angel), Satan had certain rights of approach to the throne of God in heaven because <u>at this time he had not yet been defeated and judged</u>.

During the time between the temptation and fall of mankind (likely on or before c. 3800 BC) and the time when Satan first learned of the redemption plan (likely on or before c. 1446 BC to c. 1406 BC <u>when Moses wrote the Pentateuch</u>; see previous section), Satan brings accusations (see previous scripture, Revelation 12:10) before God that mankind is immersed in sin and unredeemable (and the accusations were not groundless)—and Satan argues there is no viable plan or option for the redemption of mankind, and he (Satan) cannot be defeated. Satan was making his unrighteous case before God. (See previous section, Rebellion - Methodical, Deliberate, and Calculated.)

> It is unlikely Satan continued to bring accusations before God <u>after learning of God's plan of redemption, likely during the time of Moses (c. 1446 BC - c. 1406 BC)</u> (see end of previous section), but planned and attempted actions against the Hebrew people to seize control.

But now in this section of the book we briefly leap ahead to chapter 8 (Defeating Evil) with the birth of Jesus (1 BC) and Satan's defeat and final eviction from heaven (Luke 8:30, 10:18; 2 Peter 2:4; Revelation 12:9-12) tied to the birth, life, death, and resurrection of the Messiah, Jesus Christ.

When Jesus *was "lifted up from the earth,"* Satan's earthly kingdom **was fully defeated** at the Cross of Calvary (John 12:31-32; Revelation 12:9-12). Satan could no longer obtain access to God as before, and it was now impossible for Satan to actively accuse mankind before God's throne in Heaven. (Brace, R.A.)

Satan's defeat at Calvary and his final eviction from heaven will eventually lead to the future Great Tribulation (John 12:31). Although Satan has been defeated, he has not yet been judged by God—but ultimately, he will be judged and confined to hell for eternity (Revelation 20:10). Today we are very close to the 'tipping point' of the future seven year tribulation period (Revelation 6-19).

For more information see book, *World in Denial—Defiant Nature of Mankind (Prophetic Evidence for a Divine Creator)*, chapters 8 – 12, which document the rebellious nature of mankind and the coming Seven Year Tribulation Period. Also see the epilogue of this book, Evil Still Exists in Our World.

The Fall of the Rebel Angels; right hand panel of Hieronymus Bosch's The Haywain Triptych, (c. 1450-1516)

Michael casts out rebel angels. Illustration by Gustave Doré (1832 - 1883) for John Milton's Paradise Lost

Chapter 5

Fall of Mankind

> *"When the woman saw that the fruit of the tree was good for food and pleasing to the eye, and also desirable for gaining wisdom, she took some and ate it. She also gave some to her husband, who was with her, and he ate it."* — Genesis 3:6, NIV

Now we take a step back to chapter 3, section titled Creation and Purpose of Mankind

Fruit of all the trees in Eden was provided for Adam and Eve to eat except the fruit from one tree: the tree of the knowledge of good and evil. *"And the Lord made all kinds of trees out of the ground—trees that were pleasing to the eye and good for food. In the middle of the garden were the tree of life and the tree of the knowledge of good and evil"* (Genesis 2:9, NIV).

God told Adam <u>before Eve was created</u> that *"You are free to eat from any tree in the garden, but you must not eat from the tree of the knowledge of good and evil, for when you eat of it you will surely die"* (Genesis 2:17, NIV). This was a test of Adam's "free will" to either choose for God or against God—<u>remember that without freedom, there is no love</u>.

> The Fall of Man is described in Genesis 3. The *"tree of the knowledge of good and evil"* was placed in the garden as a "free will" test—a test of Adam's love and obedience to God. There was nothing special (supernatural) about the fruit except that Adam was told not to eat of that particular tree.

Sometime later God created Eve from the rib of Adam (Genesis 2:19-20), and we can rightly assume that God and Adam warned Eve of the forbidden tree because she knew it was forbidden. Satan (formally Lucifer, the

> There are multitudes of verses in the Bible supporting "free will"—among them, Genesis 2:16-17, 3:5; Joshua 24:15; Psalm 119:30; Isaiah 7:15, 66:3; Ezekiel 33:11; Matthew 16:24; Romans 10:13; 1 Corinthians 7:37; 2 Peter 3:9; and Revelation 22:17. For example:
>
> Moses forewarns the Israelites before setting out for the land of Canaan, *"...I have set before you life and death, blessings and curses. Now choose life, so that you and your children may live..."* (Deut. 30:19-20, NIV).
>
> Joshua 24:15 (NIV) proves that man is a free moral agent: *"...choose for yourselves this day whom you will serve."*
>
> <u>"Free will"</u> simply means "the ability of an individual to make his or her personal choice for or against God, and it is an indisputable fact of Scripture." (Hagee, p. 145-146)

Cherub angel) takes the form of a serpent (Satan begins controlling the serpent) and tempts Eve with a question:

> *"Did God really say, 'You must not eat from any tree in the garden?' The woman said to the serpent, 'We may eat fruit from the trees in the garden, but God did say, You must not eat fruit from the tree that is in the middle of the garden, and you must not touch it, or you will die'"* (Genesis 3:1-3, NIV).

Expulsion from the Garden of Eden

Adam and Eve driven out of the Garden of Eden, as imagined by the artist Gustav Dore. (Public domain image.)

This question, *"Did God really say, 'You must not eat from any tree in the garden?'"* (verse 1), suggests that God could be wrong, or He may have other motives, and then in verses 3-4, **Satan blatantly lies and tells Eve that she will not die.** *"You will not surely die,'" the serpent said to the woman. For God knows that when you eat of it your eyes will be opened, and you will be like God, knowing good and evil"* (Genesis 3:4-5, NIV).

This caused the woman to doubt what God had said—and Eve began to think that perhaps God was concealing something "good" by forbidding her (and Adam) from eating this specific fruit. Satan told Eve that if she eats the fruit of the forbidden tree she will have great wisdom and power—she would become like God.

This was a **temptation of pride—a sin of arrogance, superiority, and self-importance** (like most people in the world today). And then in an act of disobedience, Eve became convinced it was good to "know good and evil" and felt compelled to eat the fruit from the forbidden tree. Eve opened the door to her spiritual pride (thinking of the possibility of becoming like God), and then she offered the fruit to Adam and he ate the fruit as well.

"When the woman saw that the fruit of the tree was good for food and pleasing to the eye, and also desirable for gaining wisdom, she took some and ate it. She also gave some to her husband, who was with her, and he ate it" (Genesis 3:6, NIV).

> Satan is a creature of **pride** (arrogance, conceit, and self-importance). **Pride** is one of the first personality traits people recognize in other people but it is the <u>very last thing we recognize in ourselves</u>.

Satan succeeded in persuading Eve to trust him, while doubting and disobeying God, their Heavenly Father. **Adam was more culpable in his disobedience (sin) because he was warned directly by God not to eat from the tree, but he disobeyed God anyway. Adam was not misled by the serpent, but rather, he completely understood his disobedience to God in accepting the fruit from Eve** (Timothy 2:14). Like Eve, Adam opened the door to his **spiritual pride** by accepting the fruit. Adam knew the fruit was forbidden but **he chose to disobey God anyway.**

> Remember that <u>God had already told Adam before Eve was created that</u> *"you must not eat from the tree of the knowledge of good and evil, for when you eat of it you will surely die"* (Genesis 2:17, NIV).

The question (Genesis 3:1-6) posed by Satan (verse 1); the response by Eve (verses 2-3); and Satan's response that she will not die but you will be like God (verses 4-5) was the temptation—and then the touching and eating of the forbidden fruit by both Adam and Eve were **acts of defiance and disobedience** (verse 6). This was a "free will" test of choosing between good and evil. (See p. 63.) They chose to disobey God and consequently, **sin and evil infiltrated humanity** which changed the course of human history.

> God was their Heavenly Father and Creator and mentor—Adam and Eve had been walking and talking with God for many years (perhaps a hundred years or more), and they had a direct, loving relationship with Him as children today have with a loving father.
>
> If God said something was forbidden, they were expected to obey God, certainly for their own well-being. God wanted them to put their total trust and faith in Him. This was an easy test of their "free will" to choose to obey, trust, and love God. They were not children, but intelligent and good, but **they chose otherwise—they chose to disobey God, their Creator.**

> Eve was deceived but Adam was not. Adam was more culpable—he was more responsible because 1) Adam was created first and Eve was created from Adam, 2) God had previously told Adam not to eat of the tree before Eve was created, and Adam sinned knowingly and with intent, and 3) he was the one who was to lead.

> Even today **Satan still tempts gullible man** into believing he does not need God but **he can become like God by deciding his own moral standards of right and wrong behavior. The Moral Law (The Ten Commandments) has been cast aside in public schools and government institutions** in favor of man's *immoral and depraved standard of behavior.* See Appendix D, last section, The Moral Law.

Adam and Eve knew that it was morally and intellectually wrong to disobey God by eating of that particular tree, the *"tree of the knowledge of good and evil."* However, when they chose to willfully disobey God, they understood evil **because they were now separated from God.** They immediately felt the curses from God (consequences of disobedience; God withdrawing His blessings; judgment from God) and understood good and evil—**and at that point in time, sin entered humanity.**

Although it was Eve who first sinned, yet in Romans 5:12, 18, and 1 Corinthians 15:22 **the Bible lays the guilt solely on Adam.** Ultimately, the responsibility rests with Adam because he was first to be created (Eve was from Adam), **all mankind descended from Adam,** and **Adam was told directly by God not to eat from the tree. He was to show leadership and wisdom and moral courage, but instead of believing God and placing his full trust in Him, Adam blindly followed the lead of Eve.**

What made this disobedience even worse is that **neither Adam nor Eve assumed any responsibility for their actions—just like many in the world today, they shifted the blame to someone or something else—and neither Adam nor Eve repented of their sin. If they had repented, the outcome for them and their descendants (humanity) may have been different** (consequences, as detailed in the following sections, **may have been much less severe or they would likely have been forgiven), but there was no remorse. Adam and Eve hid from God** (Genesis 3:8-10), **and humanity has been hiding from God (avoiding God) ever since.**

Rather than admit their moral disobedience and ask for forgiveness, **they passed the blame to another** (Genesis 3:12-13) **as so many do when they get caught committing an offense or crime.** "From their actions in Genesis 3:7-8 and Job's statement in Job 31:33, we know **Adam tried to conceal rather than confess his sin**" (Deffinbaugh, p. 3). [Bold added]

Many theologians believe that if Adam and Eve had obeyed God, if they had remained faithful to their Creator and chosen what was good and right, the "free will" test for them and their descendants would have been fulfilled—but this is now a moot point. Some theologians, however, believe that all descendants would continue to have "free will" and evil would have persisted, and evil would have had to be defeated at the Cross.

God foreknew the problem with free will (freedom of choice), love, and evil. **The problem can be briefly restated as follows:** Without "free will" there is no love but "free will" also makes evil possible, and because God's nature is completely opposed to evil (sin), then God had to eliminate evil without destroying free will, love, and mankind who is immersed in sin (immorality, depravity, violence, lawlessness, pride, greed, and idolatry).

Lucifer was convinced that God had **no viable solution** to the problem of "free will" which makes evil possible—that is, there was **no solution to defeat evil without destroying freedom, love, and mankind** who would eventually be completely immersed in sin—and believing this to be true, **he thought he had an infallible plan to rule the earth (mankind) and the first and second heavens.**

Some may ask, what about humans in a sinless heaven? Were they given a "free will" choice? Yes—humans in heaven are redeemed—**their "free will" test was fulfilled while on earth by making the choice for God and accepting the free gift of pardon through Jesus Christ.** Once in heaven, you cannot sin. See chapter 8, God's Provision for Sin.

As Dr. Norman L. Geisler states, "One cannot get to the Promised Land without going through the wilderness. Earth is the testing ground; heaven is our final home. We cannot reach home without the proving grounds" (Geisler, p. 63-64). For more information, see chapter 8, section Best Possible Solution and section Planet Earth - God's Testing Ground.

God foreknew the problem with free will (freedom of choice), love, and evil. (See p. 63.) "God permitted Satan's influence and knew exactly the choice humanity [Adam and Eve] would make under those circumstances. But God did not force Adam and Eve to choose evil." God does not tempt (James 1:13) but, rather, **He was the author of the "free will" test to choose between good and evil.** (Alcorn, p. 239)

The immediate effects of their disobedience (sin) was spiritual death—which meant separation from God whose nature is holy and sinless (holy: Isaiah 6:1-3, 57:15; Psalm 5:5-6, 99:5; Habakkuk 1:13; and Leviticus 20:26, 11:45; and sinless: Isaiah 53:59; 1 Peter 1:18-19, 2:22; 2 Corinthians 5:21; Hebrews 4:15; Luke 1:35; 1 John 3:5; Matthew 27:24; and John 19:4, 8:29)—the source of everlasting life. (See chapter 1, Who Is God?) An impediment (barrier) between man and God was created (Romans 3:23-24)—man was now separated from God.

"The effects of sin is [sic] always separation from God. This does not mean that God does not love us, but it means God by His nature [uncompromising holiness and righteousness] must be separated from sin." Adam and Eve were now cut off from their source of life (God) and they faced an uncertain world and eventual physical death (Romans 6:23). (Goldberg, p. 5)

God created man (male and female) in His image and gave man dominion over the entire world (Genesis 1:26-28, 5:1-2). God created a perfect world (Genesis 1:31)—no death, struggle, violence, cruelty, or bloodshed—and everything was "upheld" by God (Colossians 1:17 and Hebrews 1:3). God also allowed man to be a free moral being—that is, He gave man the ability "to choose what is true, what is right, what is good." (Johnson, p. 8-10)

Defeating Evil - God's Plan Before the Beginning of Time

Expulsion from the Garden of Eden
Author: Thomas Cole (1828)

The Savage State from the Course of Empire
Author: Thomas Cole (1834)

Painting by Michelangelo (1475-1564) in the Sistine Chapel.

Immediate Effects of the Fall

Before sin entered the world, the world was good (Genesis 1:31). God "upheld" and continuously restored everything in the beginning (Colossians 1:17 and Hebrews 1:3), but when sin entered the world (through the first man, Adam—Genesis 3:6), God cursed the world (Genesis 3:14–19; God withdrew His blessings), and the perfect creation began to degenerate—that is, suffer death and decay (Romans 5:12, 6:23, 8:22; James 1:15; 1 Corinthians 11:28-30).

The dominion of man (male and female) over the entire world (Genesis 1:26-28, 5:1-2) meant that when Adam sinned, all of creation was cursed as well. Creatures under man's rule, though morally innocent, shared in God's judgment. The Curse (consequences of disobedience; God withdrawing His blessings; judgment from God) ended Creation and initiated the unfettered reign of the First and Second Laws of Thermodynamics, laws which we experience today in the form of decay and degeneration. **The laws of thermodynamics are overwhelming scientific evidence supporting the validity of creation and the curse, and the truth of Scripture**.

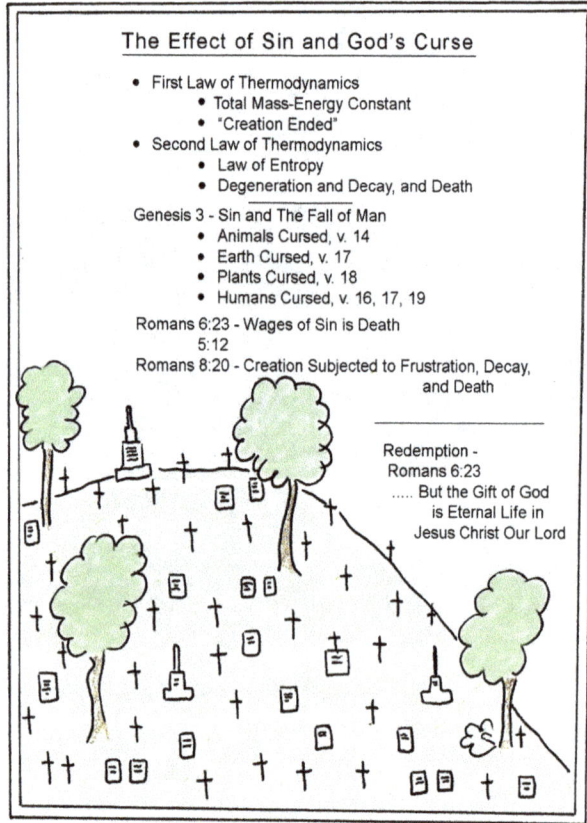

Aging and Death Are Implicit in the Second Law of Thermodynamics. *Sketch by Roger Gallop*

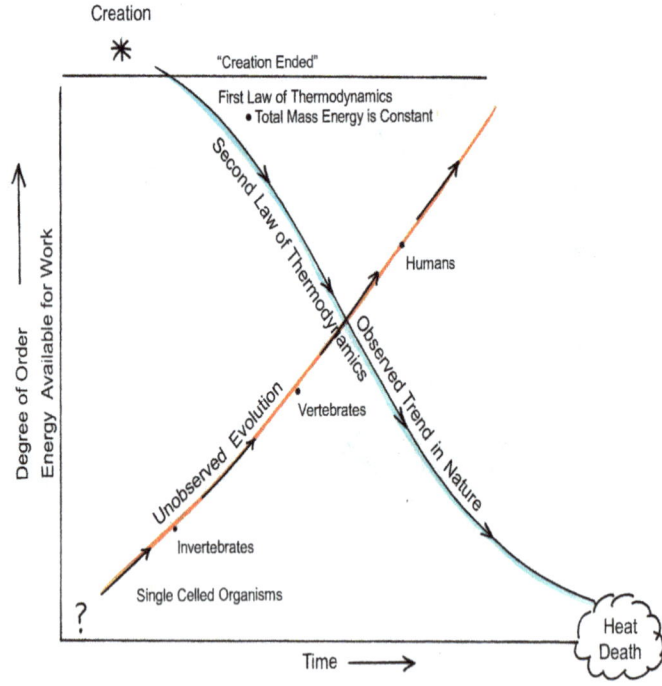

Creation, Entropy, and Heat Death
First and Second Laws of Thermodynamics Support Creation–Not Evolution
Sketch by Roger Gallop

Defeating Evil - God's Plan Before the Beginning of Time

> The **First Law of Thermodynamics** states that matter/energy cannot be created or destroyed. **Creation happened in the past but it is not happening today.**
> The **Second Law of Thermodynamics** states that matter/energy in the universe available for work is decaying or running down. This, of course, is contrary to the "chaos to cosmos, all by itself" false doctrine of evolution. The universal tendency of things to run down and to fall apart shows the universe had to be "wound up" at the start. The universe is winding down—it is not eternal. (Thaxton, C.B.)
>
> An easy to understand explanation of the First and Second Laws of Thermodynamics (decay and deterioration) are found in chapters 2 and 3 in the book by Roger Gallop, *evolution – The Greatest Deception in Modern History (Scientific Evidence for Divine Creation).*

> There was no death in the animal kingdom until Adam sinned—and with the original sin (Genesis 3), so entered death as verified in Romans 6:23 (KJV), *"For the wages of sin is death, but the gift of God is eternal life in Christ Jesus our Lord."* (cf. Romans 5:12, 8:22; James 1:15; 1 Corinthians 11:28-30)
>
> All physical evil in today's world is the result of the fall—Adam's "free will" choice to disobey God resulted in death, pain, and suffering, and disease (genetic burden is the cause of almost all disease we see today) as described in chapter 3 in the above referenced book.

The degeneration and dying process started slowly in the beginning because of zero mutational load with Adam and Eve. Cain was the firstborn to Adam and Eve, and he would have received perfect genes from his parents because the effects of sin and the Curse were nonexistent in the beginning. Mutational load we observe today is scientific evidence for 6,000 years of genetic burden and is the primary source of diseases and deformities, aging, and eventual death.

Most physical evil we see today is a result of Adam's original sin (without repentance) which resulted in genetic burden (disease) and physical and spiritual death. All physical evils (except divine judgments) can be traced back to the sin of Adam (the first human)—a free will choice. Although Lucifer committed the first sin, he was not human but a created angel in spirit form, and God will deal with Lucifer and his legion of demons in another way.

Physical and Spiritual Death

Man's death was both physical and spiritual. When Adam sinned he died spiritually by being cut off from God, the source of life. Sin works its way into the lives of all men who eventually die. Romans 6:23 (NIV), states *"For the wages of sin is death, but the gift of God is eternal life in Christ Jesus our Lord."*

Man is given time here on earth to experience life and to make a "free will" choice for or against God by accepting or rejecting the free gift of pardon offered by the Son of God, Jesus Christ. "Free will" will have been fulfilled during our life on earth (1 Corinthians 13:12; Revelation 21:1-5). This is explained in chapter 8, Defeating Evil.

Preserving love and defeating evil (remembering there is no love without freedom, but freedom makes evil possible) and maintaining a sinless heaven (where no one can sin) **must be settled before heaven**. Dr. Norman L. Geisler states, "...God has to create free creatures who could sin before He could produce free creatures who can't sin." (Geisler, p. 62) Again, see chapter 8, Defeating Evil.

Physical and Spiritual Death: In Romans 6:23 (KJV), it states, *"the wages of sin is death"*—a physical and spiritual death. Physical death is necessary for the atonement of sin. In Hebrews 9:22, NIV, *"In fact, the law requires that nearly everything be cleansed with blood, and without the shedding of blood there is no forgiveness."* As described in Hebrews 2:14-18, the death of Jesus Christ on the cross and His resurrection brought reconciliation (restored harmony) between God and mankind.

In John 11:25-26 (NIV), Jesus said, *"I am the resurrection and the life. He who believes in me will live, even though he dies; and whoever lives and believes in me will never die."* To avoid eternal spiritual death, we must personally accept the free gift of salvation by recognizing the Lord Jesus Christ as our personal Savior. This is a recurrent theme throughout the New Testament. (See John 3:16, 5:24, 14:6; Romans 10:9, 13; and Ephesians 2:8-9.)

The spirit is that part of humans that is able to love and experience God directly—it allows humans (and angels) to have a relationship with the Creator. The soul and spirit are connected but separate (Hebrews 4:12)—**the soul is who we are, but the spirit connects us with God.** Spiritual death results in eternal separation from God. See chapter 3, section, Uniqueness of Human Beings, in the book, *evolution – The Greatest Deception in Modern History (Scientific Evidence for Divine Creation)*.

In Genesis 3:15, man had forsaken God, but God had not forsaken man. A Savior was promised, He would come, and all who would accept God's provision for atonement by faith would be saved—not be taken into the "second death" but be saved from eternal separation from God. See next section, Individual Curses on Humanity.

Because of the Fall, death became a reality for all creation. All men die, all animals die, and all plant life dies. The *"whole creation groans"* (Romans 8:22, NIV) waiting for Christ to return to liberate the world from the effects of death. Because of sin, death is an unavoidable reality, and no one is immune.

"Physical death is a fearful and terrible judgment, bringing all that we have, love, and are in this world to an unhappy end. But spiritual death—alienation from God...and **God alienated from us because of our sin—is much more fearsome, leading finally (if we do not repent) to the** *second death*: **...torment in hell forever** (Matthew 25:41; Hebrews 9:27; Revelation 14:10-11, 20:14-15)." (Arnaud, p. 32) (See Appendix C.)

> **We will all die, but if we die without Christ and without accepting the gift of salvation (when Jesus bore the sins of humanity on the cross), we will experience eternal or spiritual death. And this one fact alone cannot be stated more passionately or more fervently.**

"Another effect of the Fall is that humans have lost sight of the purpose for which they were created [see chapter 3]. **Man's chief end and highest purpose in life is to glorify [praise and honor] God and enjoy Him forever [that is, to become part of God's family]** (Romans 11:36; 1 Corinthians 6:20, 10:31; Psalm 86:9). Hence, **love of God is the core of all morality and goodness.**" The opposite is arrogance and pride—"the choice of self as supreme." [Bold added] Pride (self-centeredness) is the essence of the Fall and "what follows are all the crimes against God [and humanity]." (Got questions)

> Sin is choosing otherwise; turning away from God, thus making evil possible. "We call attention to ourselves and to our good qualities and accomplishments" in life, and **we often blame others for our shortcomings. In short we place ourselves and material wealth (e.g., money, car, house, possessions, social status, etc.) above all else including Go**d. (Got questions)

When Adam chose to disobey God, "he lost his innocence, incurred the penalty of physical and spiritual death, and his mind was darkened by sin, as are the minds of his successors [descendants]" that followed. The apostle Paul said of pagans, *"Since they do not think it worthwhile to retain the knowledge of God, He gave them over to a depraved mind"* (Romans 1:28). **This is true of most of the world today.** (Got questions) See book by Roger Gallop, *World in Denial – Defiant Nature of Mankind (Prophetic Evidence for a Divine Creator)*.

The sinful nature of man escalated ("like an unstoppable deadly virus") and produced **a state of depravity within the heart of man.** Paul spoke of those *"whose consciences have been seared"* (1 Timothy 4:2, NIV) and whose minds are spiritually darkened while rejecting the truth for *"they neither glorified him as God nor gave thanks to him, but their thinking became futile and their foolish hearts were darkened..."* (Romans 1:21, NIV). In this state man is completely incapable of doing what is right and good before God. *"...the sinful mind is hostile to God. It does not submit to God's law, nor can it do so"* (Romans 8:7, NIV). (Arnaud, p. 27; Got Questions)

Individual Curses on Humanity

Lasting consequences resulted from the fall of man in the Garden of Eden. In addition to degeneration, decay, and death associated with the fall, individual curses (consequences of disobedience; God withdrawing His blessings; judgment from God) also fell not only upon Adam and Eve but upon all their offspring and, ultimately, upon the entire world throughout the course of history. Paul speaks in Romans and in 1 Corinthians of the on-going effects of Adam's sin and the ultimate cure through Christ in Romans 5:12, 19 and 1 Corinthians 15:20-22.

Romans 5:12, 19 (NIV) states, *"Therefore, just as sin came into the world through one man, and death through sin, and in this way death spread to all men, because all sinned... through the disobedience of the one man* [Adam] *the many were made sinners, so also through the obedience of the one man* [Jesus] *the many will be made righteous."*

Individual curses were pronounced on Satan (the serpent), Eve, and Adam. (Deffinbaugh, p. 4-5)

Satan (the serpent)

1) **first curse**, all the days of his life, the serpent (this creature is the embodiment of Satan) would crawl on its belly and eat dust (Genesis 3:14),

2) **second curse**, in Genesis 3:15 (NIV), God put enmity between the woman and the serpent, *"And I will put enmity between you and the woman* [Eve], *and between your offspring* [Satan's seed] *and hers* [her Seed; Jesus]." God desires no alliance with Satan, and the two (God and Satan) are mutually exclusive, and woman would flee from him (the serpent) on sight. See p. 222, item #18 regarding Genesis 3:15 in the book by Roger Gallop, *World in Denial – Defiant Nature of Mankind (Prophetic Evidence for a Divine Creator)*, and

3) **third curse**, Satan is destroyed, *"He shall crush your head, and you shall strike His heel."* God forecasts the defeat of Satan by the incarnation (God in human form) of Christ, the Messiah. The battle lines were drawn between God and Satan. *"He shall crush your head"* is a mortal wound. The power of Satan is crushed by the Cross of Christ. *"And you shall strike* [bruise] *His heel"* refers to the sacrifice of Jesus at the Cross. (See Isaiah 53:10.)

At the fall of man (when man turned away from God in the Garden of Eden), **God promised a solution to their sin. Sin was the reason for Christ going to the Cross, and at the Cross Christ crushed Satan's head. Christ not only fully paid for the sins of the world on the Cross but He defeated Satan as well** (Colossians 2:14-15).

"In Genesis 3:15 we find the first prediction relative to the Savior of the world, called 'the seed of the woman.' In the original oracle God foretold the age-long conflict which would be waged between the 'seed of the woman' [Jesus Christ, Lord and Savior] and 'the seed of the serpent' [Satan] and which will eventually be won by the 'seed of the woman.' This primitive promise indicates a struggle between the Messiah of Israel, the Savior of the world, on the one hand, and Satan, the adversary of the human soul, on the other. It foretells complete victory eventually for the Messiah." (McDowell, p. 151)

See chapter 8, Defeating Evil, for a more expansive explanation of how Satan was destroyed at the Cross.

Eve

Her sin involved the act of doubting and disobeying God, and also acting freely (separately) from her husband and then shifting the blame to the serpent (Genesis 3:13). Her deliverance would be through her "seed" (Jesus) who would crush the serpent's head. The process through which her deliverance came would be painful to her seed (the bruised heel – Jesus' sacrifice on the cross). The curses on Eve are the following:

1) **first curse**, child-bearing would be a painful experience. Labor pains were a part of Eve's curse and for all women throughout history who experience childbirth (Genesis 3:16), and

2) **second curse**, she is to be ruled over by her husband (Genesis 3:16). Originally, God created Eve to be her husband's partner or coworker, not to be "ruled over." We must remember that Adam's headship, even before the fall, was based on being created first (his prior existence) and the fact that Eve was created from his flesh. (See 1 Corinthians 11:3-12, especially 8-12.)

Adam

Rather than lead, Adam followed Eve, and **disobeyed God when God told Adam before Eve was created tha**t *"... you must not eat from the tree of the knowledge of good and evil, for when you eat of it you will surely die"* (Genesis 2:17, NIV); and then to make matters worse, **Adam shifted the blame to Eve** (Genesis 3:12). Adam is more responsible (guilty or culpable) in his sin and is cursed with a different type of labor pain.

1) **first curse**, he would have to labor, fight, and scrap for everything which the land reluctantly yields to him (and this is exactly what has happened to man throughout history), and

2) **second curse**, he (and she who is from Adam) would ultimately succumb to the ground (death).

Chapter 6

Effects of Evil on Humanity

> *"Then the Lord saw that the wickedness of man was great on the earth, and that every intent of the thoughts of his heart was only evil continually. And the Lord was sorry that He had made man on the earth, and He was grieved in His heart. And the Lord said, 'I will blot out man whom I have created from the face of the land, from man to animals to creeping things and to birds of the sky; for I am sorry that I have made them.'"* — Genesis 6:5-7, NAS

In addition to the curses pronounced by God on mankind, Adam and Eve's disobedience opened the door to evil—and with evil came ensuing pain, suffering, decay, disease, and physical and spiritual death (Romans 6:23-24)—and spiritual death meant separation from God, the source of life.

Free will makes evil possible—and in a free world, not all will freely choose good, but many people will choose evil. Given that we are free human beings, even an all-powerful, loving God is unable to reasonably persuade all to choose the right path—the path to life and goodness. God cannot act coercively or forcibly but only persuasively. A God of love cannot force people to love Him—to love goodness.

How did evil affect humanity? Sin and rebellion are contagious—a slippery slope downhill. Evil infiltrates the lives of everyone (like mutational load or genetic burden described in chapter 3 of the book, *evolution - The Greatest Deception in Modern History (Scientific Evidence for Divine Creation)*. Its effect is never confined to just one person—sin continues to grow worse and spreads like an "unstoppable, deadly virus"—it permeates mankind who becomes more sinful and depraved over time. (Arnaud, p. 27)

Evil is not a thing, object, or substance but rather it is a corruption of something good such as "free will." Evil is like a wound or disease in the arm or rot in a tree. "Evil is a real corruption [decay] but it is not a real thing (substance)...it does not exist in and of itself." (Geisler, p. 20)

The human arm or a tree are good things but corruption, decay and deterioration, and disease are the result of the second law of thermodynamics and mutational load (genetic burden) which, in turn, is the result of sin in the world. See chapter 5, Immediate Effects of the Fall.

Moral evil is simply choosing not to obey God—which in turn leads to physical evil with its ensuing pain, suffering, decay (deterioration), disease and death. Physical evil is the result of moral evil (disobeying God; the Moral Law) in some way.

Physical evil can be defined in terms of immorality, lawlessness, violence, depravity, corruption, and persecution. In today's world, evil resides in the hearts of all men (Genesis 6:5; Jeremiah 7:19).

The history of mankind, especially God's people (the Jews), is clearly detailed in the book, *World in Denial - Defiant Nature of Mankind (Prophetic Evidence for a Divine Creator)*. This book bears witness to the continuous sinfulness—violence and depravity of mankind.

Defiant Antediluvian (Pre-Flood) People
(4004 BC - 2385 BC)

When Adam and Eve sinned they deliberately and purposefully disobeyed God, a sin that should never have been committed—and from this one sinful act, they lost their innocence and were now cut off from their Creator and source of life. Genesis 4 and 5 depict a graveyard of sinful humanity and by chapter 6 of Genesis, the whole earth had become completely and utterly corrupt (immoral and depraved) requiring judgment of the flood. (For more information, see book, *evolution - The Greatest Deception in Modern History*, chapters 4 - 6, and 10.)

It is important to understand the state of affairs during the 1,600-year antediluvian (pre-flood) period. Because of the fall of Adam and Eve, human beings had acquired the knowledge of good and evil (Genesis 3:7, 22); more specifically, the knowledge of evil. This was the Age of Conscience, the second of the seven ages or dispensations—God's method of dealing with humanity throughout history. (See book *evolution - The Greatest Deception in Modern History*, p. 212, end note 6, and book, *World in Denial - Defiant Nature of Mankind*, p. xii, Preface.)

During this time, people had no institution of government and law and could only distinguish between good and evil by their own conscience and personal Divine revelations. Mankind was given the individual and moral responsibility to pursue goodness and virtue and turn away from evil.

God provided man with a means of atonement; that is, animals were allowed to be sacrificed and their blood shed so mankind could be reconciled to their Creator. However, during this period, humanity abandoned its relationship with God—and ultimately, they were consumed with wickedness and violence continually. *"Now the earth was corrupt in the sight of God, and the earth was filled with violence"* (Genesis 6:11, NAS). The human race became morally depraved, which is thoroughly described in Genesis 6.

> *"Then the Lord saw that the wickedness of man was great on the earth, and that every intent of the thoughts of his heart was only evil **continually**. And the Lord was sorry that He had made man on the earth, and He was grieved in His heart. And the Lord said, **'I will blot out man whom I have created from the face of the land, from man to animals to creeping things and to birds of the sky; for I am sorry that I have made them'***** (Genesis 6:5-7, NAS). [Bold added]

> *"Now the earth was corrupt in the sight of God, and the earth was filled with violence. And God looked on the earth, and behold, it was corrupt; for all flesh had corrupted their way upon the earth"* (Genesis 6:11-12, NAS).

W. Graham Scroggie has graphically depicted the biblical picture of antediluvian humanity. (Scroggie, p. 74, 77)

> The appalling condition of things is summed up in a few terrible words, words which bellow and burn: wickedness, evil imagination, corruption, and violence; and these sins were great, widespread, 'in the earth,' continuous, 'only evil continually,' open and daring, 'before God,' replete, 'filled,' and universal, 'all flesh.'... This is an astounding event! After over 1,600 years of human history the race was so utterly corrupt morally that it was not fit to live; and of all mankind only four men and four women were spared, because they did not go with the great sin drift.

This period had reached a point of continuous utter depravity. The degradation and wickedness of the antediluvians have been affirmed by an astonishing collection of Scriptural testimony (Genesis 6:1-6, 11-13; Luke 17:26-27; 1 Peter 3:20; 2 Peter 2:5; and Jude 14-15). In the days of Noah (4004 BC–2385 BC), mankind was rebellious and exceedingly and brazenly wicked—and with this rebellion and wickedness came eventual consequences—the Flood that destroyed humanity.

An Important Prophetic Message to Mankind in Today's World

As in the 'days of Noah' when the 'tipping point' (the measure of sin) was reached, God saved a righteous family from the flood. Jesus said that in the last days (the final days just before the Second Coming of Jesus Christ), *"...iniquity [lawlessness] shall abound, the love of many shall wax cold"* (Matthew 24:2, KJV). In today's world, the measure of sin is abounding exponentially. Read 2 Peter 3:3-7 about the parallels of the Flood and the coming war of Armageddon. (Hal Lindsey, November 6, 2015)

Today, the whole Creation groans and travails as the world becomes "normalized" (desensitized) to lawlessness, depravity, moral decay, political corruption, and violence—for example, daily violence in Chicago, Detroit, Baltimore, Los Angeles, and in many other cities throughout the U.S. including mass shootings in elementary schools and high schools across America over the last few decades (e.g., the shooting on February 14, 2018, at Marjory Stoneman Douglas High School in Parkland, Broward County, Florida, where 17 students lost their lives at the hands of a deranged gunman and former student). Most people know that something is morally WRONG with America and the world. See the book, *World in Denial - Defiant Nature of Mankind (Prophetic Evidence for a Divine Creator)*, chapters 9 and 10.

God has been long-suffering and tolerant in his judgment of the U.S. and the world, but the time is coming when the "measure of sin is now full." (See Genesis 15:16.) Today we are very close to the 'tipping point' of the seven year tribulation but the world seems oblivious to the reality of such events:

> *"...though seeing, they may not see; though hearing, they may not understand"* (Luke 8:10-12, NIV). Paul spoke of those *"whose consciences have been seared"* (1 Timothy 4:2, NIV) and whose minds are spiritually darkened while rejecting the truth for *"they neither glorified him as God nor gave thanks to him, but their thinking became futile and their foolish hearts were darkened..."* (Romans 1:21, NIV; see Romans 8:7, NIV). This describes much of the world today.

For more information see books: *evolution – The Greatest Deception in Modern History (Scientific Evidence for Divine Creation)*, chapters 4 - 6, and 10, The Antediluvian Period; and *World in Denial—Defiant Nature of Mankind (Prophetic Evidence for a Divine Creator)*, chapters 9 - 12, which documents the rebellious nature of mankind and the coming Seven Year Tribulation.

Worldwide Flood
Restructuring of Pangaea
(2385 BC)

In the early 20th century, Alfred Wegener, a German meteorologist, noted that the continents (including the continental shelves) fit together as a single supercontinent. This antediluvian (pre-flood) landmass is commonly called Pangaea, from the Greek root word for "all lands." The northern part of Pangaea is called Laurasia, and the southern part is called Gondwanaland. Refer back to chapter 3 for a larger map of Pangaea.

The separation or splitting apart of this ancient landmass took place about 4,400 years ago during a catastrophic worldwide flood—a global event described in Genesis 6-8. This catastrophic shifting of landmasses and flooding took place within a span of just one year—NOT millions of years as maintained by uniformitarian, secular geologists. There is abundant, overwhelming physical evidence in support of the splitting of the Pangaea landmass and a worldwide flood. See chapter 4, Phase Diagram of the Worldwide Flood in the book, *evolution – The Greatest Deception in Modern History,* and the **video** on the website, **www.CreationScienceToday.com**.

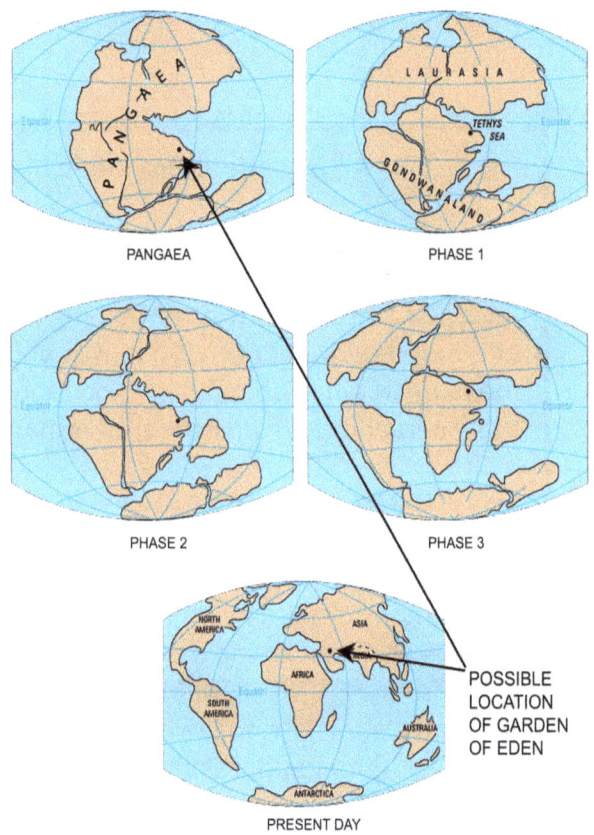

Restructuring of the earth during the worldwide flood. See map of Pangaea in chapter 3, p. 15.

Substantial geomorphic evidence supports the splitting of this ancient supercontinent. This includes not only the physiographic fit of the continents but also the alignment of major fault zones when the continents are placed together. **For many esteemed geologists who have researched geologic landforms and catastrophic processes, evidence of a global flood is indisputable.** The questions are, **how long** did it take, and **when** did the splitting occur?

Events leading to our current land features were catastrophic rifting and subduction, uplift of ocean basins, flooding of the continents, sedimentary deposition, burial of uprooted forests (creating the coal and oil we find today), mountain and continental uplift, and torrential erosional drainage by the floodwaters. Horizontal movement—seafloor spreading and continental drift—was the main tectonic force during the first phase of the flood event, and vertical movement (uplift and subsidence of ocean basins, and mountain uplift or orogeny) was predominant in the latter two phases of the flood.

See chapter 6, section Origin of Coal and Oil, p. 123, in the book, *evolution - The Greatest Deception in Modern History;* also, see p. 65 of same book, Coal and Oil – Uprooted Forests Rapidly Buried and Sealed.

According to Genesis 8:4, NIV, Noah's *"ark came to rest on the mountains of Ararat"* located in present day eastern Turkey, and Noah and his family would have soon encountered the present-day Tigris and Euphrates Rivers. As Noah and his family came off the ark, they would have named the present-day rivers with names they were most familiar with in Pangaea—and this is exactly what they did. The original Euphrates, Tigris, Pishon, and Gihon Rivers are covered over with several thousand feet of sediment deposits from the worldwide flood.

As described in Genesis 6–9, the Flood would have totally restructured the surface of the earth—no place would have been untouched by this massive flood.

The present day location of the Tigris-Euphrates River Valley contains fossiliferous sediment deposits more than several thousand feet thick from which are pumped enormous quantities of oil and gas.

Observational and empirical evidence points to the rapid formation of coal and oil as vast forests were uprooted and then buried beneath massive amounts of heated sediment worldwide during the second phase of this worldwide flood. This phenomenon is explained in chapter 6, Origin of Coal and Oil, in the book by Roger Gallop, *evolution – The Greatest Deception in Modern History (Scientific Evidence for Divine Creation)*.

The Great Flood of Noah's day (2385 BC) and future judgment are described in 2 Peter 3:3-7, NIV. Verses 5-7 state: *"But they deliberately forget that long ago by God's word the heavens existed and the earth was formed out of water and by water. By these waters also the world of that time was **deluged and destroyed**. By the same word the present heavens and earth are reserved for fire [future Armageddon], being kept for the day of judgment and destruction of ungodly men."* See the books *evolution - The Greatest Deception in Modern History*, chapter 10, Comparison to the Second Coming, and *World in Denial - Defiant Nature of Mankind*, chapter 12, Armageddon - The Great Tribulation.

Do we know the possible location of the Garden of Eden in terms of today's geography?

The approximate location of Eden in today's world can be reasonably approximated based NOT upon the location of the original four rivers (which were obliterated by the Flood), but rather upon 1) the current location of Mount Ararat, 2) the known resting place of Noah's Ark (Genesis 8:2-5), 3) the movement and geographic fit of today's continents, and 4) the names of present day rivers, Euphrates and Tigris. See map of Pangaea, pages 15 and 46.

First, Genesis 8:2-5 describes the formation of our present ocean basins and recession of water from the newly formed continents. (See **video** at www.CreationScienceToday.com.)

> *"Now the springs of the deep and the floodgates of the heavens had been closed, and the rain had stopped falling from the sky. The water receded steadily from the earth. At the end of the hundred and fifty days*

*the water had gone down, and on the seventeenth day of the seventh month the ark came to rest on the **mountains of Ararat**. The waters continued to recede until the tenth month, and on the first day of the tenth month the tops of the mountains became visible"* (Genesis 8:2-5, NIV). [Bold added]

The mountains of Ararat did not exist before the Flood. As the continents separated during the flood event (splitting, uplifting of ocean basins and sediment deposition, and uplifting of mountain ranges and subsidence of ocean basins we see today), the ark would have been pushed along in front of the original African continent as the mid-Atlantic rift separated as shown in the Pangaea drawing (chapter 3, page 15). As the ark moved along ahead of the present day African continent and came to rest on Mount Ararat, one could reasonably assume the approximate location of Eden would be in the proximity of present day Iraq—near the landmass from which it originated.

When Noah and his family eventually disembarked the ark, they faced a completely devastated earth—a mud-slick land surface, no vegetation (most of the vegetation had been buried and sealed under massive sediment deposits), great winds, cold temperatures, and a forbidding landscape. This was the beginning of the Postdiluvian Period and the Great Ice Age.

After the flood during the Ice Age (see chapter 4 in the book, *evolution - The Greatest Deception in Modern History*), it was cold and harsh—the land was devastated and denuded of vegetation, and meat could be easily preserved. Thus God allowed man to eat meat and, consequently, animals developed a fear and dread of man.

In Genesis 9:2-3, NIV, we read: *"The fear and dread of you will fall upon all the beasts of the earth and all the birds of the air, upon every creature that moves along the ground, and upon all the fish of the sea; they are given into your hands. Everything that lives and moves will be food for you. Just as I gave you the green plants, I now give you everything."*

Humans and many animal kinds became predatory—a learned trait and a form of adaptation to the post-flood environment. Natural selection (see chapter 3 in the book, *evolution - The Greatest Deception in Modern History*) allowed certain kinds of animals coming off the ark, especially those with large teeth, to gain a predatory advantage in the new world. But with superior intelligence, man was by far the most proficient hunter.

Mount Ararat, Turkey

Tigris and Euphrates Rivers in Iraq - Cradle of Civilization

Mt. Ararat, Turkey (August, 1989)

Continual Defiance of Mankind
(2384 BC - Present Day)

According to Genesis 8:4, Noah's *"ark came to rest on the mountains of Ararat"* located in present day eastern Turkey, and Noah and his family would have soon encountered the present-day Tigris and Euphrates Rivers. God commanded the descendants of Noah to *"increase in number and fill the earth"* (Genesis 9:1, NIV), but within just a few hundred years people chose to locate in the area of Mesopotamia in direct disobedience to God.

> Mesopotamia (Greek meaning "between two rivers") is an area geographically located between the present day Tigris and Euphrates rivers, corresponding to modern-day Iraq and the western part of Iran (south of Mt. Ararat). The area called Sumer in southern Mesopotamia (see map of Mesopotamia) is commonly known as the "cradle of civilization."

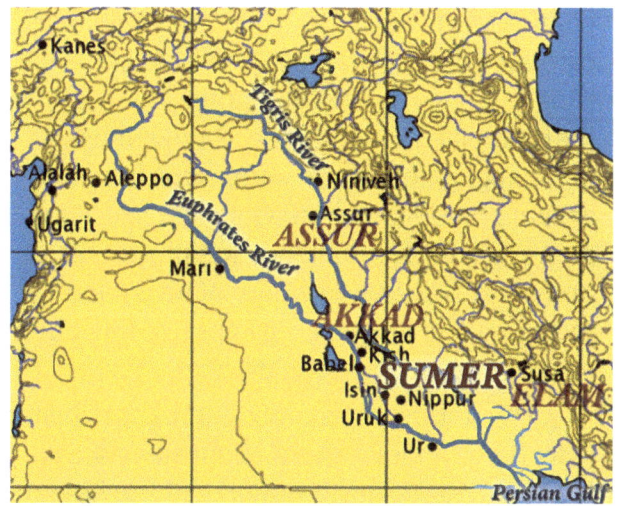
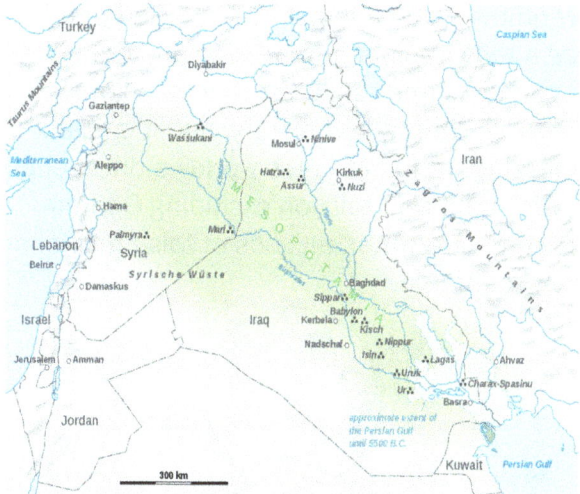

Mesopotamia; Sumer was the first urban civilization in the historical region of southern Mesopotamia, modern-day southern Iraq.

Under the rule of King Nimrod (name: "let us revolt"), the people united in building a great city called Babel (Babylon) and erected an enormous tower. The Tower of Babel (2200 BC) was not built for the worship and praise of God but rather, it was dedicated to a false man-made religion, with a motive of celebrating man's crowning achievement. This is made clear in the words of Genesis 11:4 (NIV), *"Then they said, 'Come, let us build ourselves a city, with a tower that reaches to the heavens, so that **we may make a name for ourselves** and not be scattered over the face of the whole earth.'"* [Bold added]

Note how often plaques are placed on public buildings or monuments with the names of public officials (for example, mayor, head of public works, architect, and engineer) who were in power or had a hand in the building. *"Let us make for ourselves a name"* (Genesis 11:4, NAS) is the fundamental nature of man—the nature of an arrogant

and immoral race. It exposes the sin of **Pride** and basic philosophy of humanism: "Glory to man in the highest, for man is the master of things." This is the central thought and motivation of humanism—glory to mankind.
(Stedman, p. 1)

The population that descended from Noah's family had one language and by living together in one location (Mesopotamia), they were disobeying God's command to *"fill the earth"* (Genesis 9:1). Because of this, God confused their languages and caused the people to break up into small groups and scatter throughout the earth (Genesis 11:5-9).

Why would God want to split the population into many subgroups? Because of the fallen nature of man, God knew that mankind as a centralized group would eventually rebel against the true God and begin to worship a human king and create pagan idols and religions. This has been the trend throughout history, and it is a fast-emerging trend in today's world—a one-world government and religion excluding God the Creator—but rather, all gods of false religions are acceptable.

Worshiping pagan idols and religions instead of the true God. *Sketch by Anton Zakharov*

Rebellious and idolatrous history of humanity and the natural tendency for moral decay are graphically portrayed throughout the Bible (Old and New Testaments): the paganistic cultures of the antediluvian period (c. 4004 BC to 2385 BC); the time of Mesopotamia (c. 2200 BC); ancient Egypt and Assyria (c. 2000 BC); Canaanite people of the Middle East (c. 1600 BC to 1400 BC); and the empires of Babylonia (c. 612 BC to 539 BC), Medo-Persia (c. 538 BC to 334 BC), Greece (c. 334 BC to 146 BC), and Rome (c. 146 BC to AD 476); and the historical accounts of the Dark Ages (c. 6th to 14th century), World War I and World War II; and by today's continual worldwide ethnic conflicts and threats of nuclear war.

Consider the world today with its political corruption, lying, slander, public displays of moral depravity, bizarre behavior, violent crimes against humanity, abortion, theft, adultery, drug-taking, drunkenness, gambling, greed of all kinds, prostitution, sexual perversions, trafficking of children and teenagers for sex, violence in our schools and cities, wars and rumors of wars, and terrorism. We only get a glimpse of this during national news on television.

The nature of mankind throughout history is to 'harden their hearts' (Ephesians 4:18; Mark 8:17-18). This hardening of the heart is a supernatural phenomenon, an unseen battle between good and evil we witness in the news and in our everyday lives, even with those closest to us. The evil nature of mankind is also portrayed by the exceedingly repugnant behavior of some clergymen over the ages—physical cruelty, collusion with political dictators, and abhorrent sexual abuses of children—detestable behavior that has alienated many from the Christian faith.

Immorality is tolerated and accepted as the norm by our youth. The problem has never been with God of the Holy Bible but with the corruption and moral depravity of mankind. Take a moment to read Romans 1, verses 18–32—it reads like a commentary of today's world.

> "The wrath of God is being revealed from heaven against all the godlessness and wickedness of men who suppress the truth by their wickedness, since what may be known about God is plain to them, because God has made it plain to them. For since the creation of the world God's invisible qualities—His eternal power and divine nature—have been clearly seen, being understood from what has been made, so that men are **without excuse**. For although they knew God, they neither glorified Him as God nor gave thanks to Him, but their thinking became futile and their foolish hearts were darkened" (Romans 1:18-21, NIV). [Bold added]

> "Although **they claimed to be wise, they became fools** and exchanged the glory of the immortal God for images made to look like mortal man and birds and animals and reptiles. Therefore God gave them over in the sinful desires of their hearts to sexual impurity for the degrading of their bodies with one another. **They exchanged the truth of God for a lie**, and worshiped and served created things [idols] rather than the Creator—who is forever praised. Amen. Because of this, God gave them over to **shameful lusts**. Even their women exchanged natural relations for unnatural ones [e.g., LGBT}. In the same way the **men also abandoned natural relations with women and were inflamed with lust for one another. Men committed indecent acts with other men,** and received in themselves the due penalty for their perversion" (Romans 1:22–27, NIV). [Bold added]

> "Furthermore, since they did not think it worthwhile to retain the knowledge of God, He gave them over to a depraved mind, to do what ought not to be done. **They have become filled with every kind of wickedness, evil, greed and depravity. They are full of envy, murder, strife, deceit and malice. They are gossips, slanderers, God-haters, insolent, arrogant and boastful; they invent ways of doing evil; they disobey their parents; they are senseless, faithless, heartless, ruthless.** Although they know God's righteous decree that those who do such things deserve death, they not only continue to do these very things but also approve of those who practice them" (Romans 1:28-32, NIV). [Bold added]

Other Scripture pertaining to the sinful nature of man includes the following verses.

> [5]"The LORD saw how great the wickedness of the human race had become on the earth, and that every inclination of the thoughts of the human heart was only evil all the time" (Genesis 6:5, NIV).

> [9]"The heart is deceitful above all things and beyond cure. Who can understand it?" (Jeremiah 17:9, NIV)

> [24]"But they did not listen or pay attention; instead, they followed the stubborn inclinations of their evil hearts. They went backward and not forward" (Jeremiah 7:24, NIV).

> [18]"But the things that come out of a person's mouth come from the heart, and these defile them. [19]For out of the heart come evil thoughts—murder, adultery, sexual immorality, theft, false testimony, slander" (Matthew 15:18-19, NIV).

[20]"He went on: "What comes out of a person is what defiles them. [21]For it is from within, out of a person's heart, that evil thoughts come—sexual immorality, theft, murder, [22]adultery, greed, malice, deceit, lewdness, envy, slander, arrogance and folly. [23]All these evils come from inside and defile a person" (Mark 7:20-23, NIV).

[4]"In his pride the wicked man does not seek him; in all his thoughts there is no room for God" (Psalm 10:4, NIV).

There is a deep knowing in the human psyche, a realization that something is wrong in the world today. **To the average American it is obvious that something is WRONG**—what I refer to as the "gray veil." Romans 8:22 (NIV) says that *"the whole creation groans and labors with birth pangs...."* Many believe the world is going through something akin to childbirth. That means that the labor pangs are growing in frequency and intensity as we move toward a specific event. See *World in Denial – Defiant Nature of Mankind*, p. 146 (A Deep Knowing Something is Wrong) and chapters 8 through 12.

Chapter 7

The Problem with Free Will

> *"Because of the increase in wickedness, the love of most will grow cold, but he who stands firm to the end will be saved."* — Matthew 24:12, NIV *"Woe to those who call evil good and good evil, who put darkness for light and light for darkness, who put bitter for sweet and sweet for bitter."* — Isaiah 5:20, NIV

Why didn't God create humans who would not sin? The answer is, "there is no love without freedom" and by creating humans without freedom of choice, God would simply be creating robots, but allowing "free will" also makes evil possible. If people are given a choice, some will always choose evil—they will choose against God.

Then why didn't God create mankind with "free will" but annihilate those who He knew in advance would choose to sin? This, again, would be subverting the very nature of free will—human beings free to choose for or against God. God cannot demand that you either love me or I'll annihilate you—this of course is absurd. Mankind must be free to choose, either for God or against God—and freedom to choose makes evil possible. This obviously creates a problem for God. (See page 1, Who is God?)

> God foreknew (before laying the foundations of the world) the problem with "free will" (freedom of choice), love, and evil.
>
> **The problem can be briefly restated as follows:** Without "free will" there is no love but "free will" also makes evil possible, and because God's nature is completely opposed to evil (sin), God had to eliminate evil without destroying free will, love, and mankind who is completely immersed in sin (immorality, depravity, violence, lawlessness, greed and idolatry).

Free Will Makes Evil Possible

Everyone experiences evil in their life. Evil is sin and iniquity in various forms of wickedness, immorality, depravity, violence, lawlessness, and persecution. Evil is not a real thing (an object or substance such as a car or tree) but rather **it is corruption (decay) of something good** such as a tree, a house, an automobile, or a human being (new born baby or infant). Free will is simply choosing to obey or disobey God but free will also makes evil possible.

In his book, *If God, Why Evil?*, Dr. Norman L. Geisler explains, "evil is like a wound in an arm....rot to a tree ...rust to a car.... Evil is a real corruption, but it is not a real thing (substance)." The wound, rot, or rust does not exist by itself but exists only as part of something good such as the human body, tree, or car. So "even if evil is not a thing, it's still real, and it's happening." (Geisler, p. 19-20, 22)

Another example of the corruption of something good is a young adolescent who

> **Evil** is sin or iniquity; or choosing not to obey God. The consequences of evil are pain, suffering, decay (deterioration), disease, and death.
>
> **Moral evil** is disobeying God—it is breaking the moral law (see Appendix D, last section, The Moral Law), or any one of the Ten Commandments, or a departure from goodness.
>
> **Physical evil** is immorality, lawlessness, violence, depravity, corruption, and persecution with its ensuing pain, suffering, decay, disease and death. Physical evil is the result of moral evil (disobeying God; the Moral Law) in some way. See Appendix B.
>
> Decay or deterioration and aging via the Second Law of Thermodynamics is evidence for creation and the curse (consequences for disobedience; God withdrawing His blessings; judgment from God); see chapter 5, Immediate Effects of the Fall, and chapters 2 and 3 in the book, *evolution – The Greatest Deception in Modern History.*

> Love is an intense feeling of affection. There are four forms of love: friendship (platonic), romantic, natural affection (familial), and agape. The first three can be understood in terms of shared mutual benefit that is found in all animals. And most importantly, there is no love without freedom (free will), and there is no freedom without love.
>
> "God is love" (1 John 4:8, 4:16, NIV). The word "love" in this verse is translated 'agape love' found only in humans and God (Romans 5:8)—an unconditional, self-sacrificing love. (See Prologue, Good and Evil, in the book, *World in Denial - Defiant Nature of Mankind.*)
>
> He created us to have fellowship with Him and He sacrificed His Son to restore that fellowship, *"For God so loved the world that he gave his one and only Son, that whoever believes in him shall not perish but have eternal life"* (John 3:16, NIV). (See p. 44, Forms of Life and Love, in the book, *evolution – The Greatest Deception in Modern History.*)

decides to walk into an elementary school and shoot his classmates. Those familiar with the perpetrator often say, "But he was a good boy, and he wouldn't hurt anyone." What happened? This young boy, who was once innocent and good, made the "free will" choice to commit a terrible evil. Free will makes evil possible. All acts of physical evil (see text box above) are the corruption of something good.

If we are free to love God, we are free to do otherwise, and if we are free to praise (honor) God, we are also free to defame (dishonor) God—for example, taking the Lord's name in vain which is so frequently done in the world today, <u>especially in Hollywood movies</u>. So the very nature of "free will" or freedom of choice makes evil possible because it is the power to do otherwise or turn away from God. Mankind can choose to do evil, and evil grows from bad to worse—it perpetuates itself.

God created only good things, and there is nothing evil about "free will." No one goes around protesting freedom or chanting anti-freedom slogans. Our country fought a civil war, the revolutionary war, and WWI and WWII to liberate people from slavery and oppression by evil dictators. If freedom is good, then evil is possible—evil is a corruption of something good. And remember that God knew mankind must be given a choice, otherwise we would have been created as robots, and there would be no love. (Geisler, p. 28-29; Alcorn p. 26; Bickel, p. 19-20)

God can gently persuade someone to make the right choice, but He cannot force people to love Him or freely accept Him. Love cannot force itself on another's will (conviction or belief), and we know this to be true from our everyday life and associations with other people. This is why Jesus said, *"Jerusalem, Jerusalem, you who kill the prophets and stone those sent to you, how often I have longed to gather your children together, as a hen gathers her chicks under her wings, but **you were not willing**"* (Matthew 23:37, NIV). [Bold added]

Could Evil Have Been Avoided?

Why does a good, holy and righteous God allow evil? Why doesn't God perform more miracles to avert evil, and why does He, according to the Bible, allow some people to experience pain and suffering while others do not. And although there is strong evidence that God did not create evil, He allows it to occur. Scripture tells us that God is completely sovereign—so then, why does God permit evil?

God is in complete control. *"You can do all things; no plan of yours can be thwarted"* (Job 42:2, NIV); *"Our God is in heaven; he does whatever pleases him"* (Psalm 115:3, NIV); *"The Lord does whatever pleases him, in the heavens and on the earth, in the seas and all their depths"* (Psalm 135:6, NIV); *"The king's heart is in the hand of the Lord; he directs it like a watercourse wherever he pleases"* (Proverbs 21:1, NIV).

There is nothing that happens apart from God knowing, planning, and controlling it for His purposes. Even king Nebuchadnezzar confessed that *"...the Most High is sovereign over the kingdoms of men and gives them to anyone he wishes and sets over them the lowliest of men"* (Daniel 4:17, NIV).

We know that God is all good—completely loving, just, and holy (Isaiah 6:1-3, 57:15; Psalm 5:5-6, 99:5; Habakkuk 1:13)—so why doesn't He end the pain and suffering? After all, God is almighty (Genesis 17:1; Job 5:17) and omnipotent (Romans 8:29; Ephesians 1:4-5; 1 Corinthians 2:7), and evil directly opposes His loving and holy nature (Leviticus 11:45; Isaiah 6:3; Malachi 3:6; James 1:17; Hebrews 1:10-12, 6:18).

God has the power to end evil at any time and, certainly, an all good, all-powerful God wants to do away with evil and its consequences—pain, suffering, and death. And better yet, when evil first appeared, why didn't he just do away with any possibility of evil? Again, He has the power to do so. *"For nothing is impossible with God"* (Luke 1:37, NIV), so does He lack the compassion? And when Lucifer and a third of the angels rebelled against God (chapter 4), why didn't God end wickedness soon after and bind these rebellious angels in the Abyss? These are good questions, but there are equally good answers.

Although God is completely sovereign, He has certain limitations. *"God is love"* (1 John 4:8, 4:16, NIV) but, as we know, there is no love without freedom and "free will" makes evil possible. **So could evil have been avoided? The answer is, unfortunately, No.** In this world there are always people who will choose evil (sin). Such limitations are explained in the next section.

Evil is not a thing but rather a corruption of something good such as "free will." Evil is like a wound or disease in the body or rot in a tree. "Evil is a real corruption but it is not a real thing (substance)." (Geisler, p. 19-20)

Moral evil is simply choosing not to obey God—which in turn leads to physical evil with its ensuing pain, suffering, decay (deterioration), disease, and death. Physical evil is the result of moral evil (disobeying God; the Moral Law) in some way.

In today's world, evil resides in the hearts of all men (Genesis 6:5; Jeremiah 7:19) and the tendency to do evil (turning away from God) seems to grow worse, spreading like an "unstoppable, deadly virus." (Arnaud, p. 27)

Does God Have Limitations?

We must understand that even though God is sovereign and all-powerful, He has limitations. So after all we have said about God's complete sovereignty, is this really possible? Yes—so what are some of these limitations?

God can't cease being God; He can't change who He is (God is Love; 1 John 4:8, 4:16); He can't cease being eternal (Habakkuk 1:12, 3:6); He can't lie (Hebrews 6:18); He can't sin (1 Peter 2:22; 1 John 3:5; Habakkuk 1:13); and He cannot make a square circle. And most importantly, "He cannot force anyone to *freely* accept Him" or to love Him as their Heavenly Father. "Forcing people to 'freely' believe is a contradiction in terms. God is love (1 John 4:8, 4:16), and love cannot work coercively—only persuasively." (Geisler, p. 38, 67)

Some may argue that God should have explained all of this "face to face" with humans and this would have made a difference—but that is exactly what God did with Adam and Eve who had been walking and talking with God for many years—they had a direct loving relationship with Him as children today have with a loving father. Nevertheless, they chose to disobey God without remorse—and with this sin came physical and spiritual separation from God. See chapter 5, Fall of Mankind.

We know that "free will" (freedom) makes evil possible, and people will eventually choose evil (sin). **So with "free will" could evil have been avoided? The answer is No.** In this world there will always be people who will choose evil (sin). The only way God could destroy evil is to destroy "free will" (freedom of choice), and the consequences of destroying "free will" would be to destroy the possibility to love—there is no love without freedom.

Lucifer, the fallen angel, believed God had no viable solution—that if He (God) destroyed freedom, He would be destroying love, peace, hope, beauty, and fellowship, and all mankind would be eternally separated from the Creator. As a consequence, Lucifer believed he would rule the earth, mankind, and the first and second heavens. See chapter 4, Origin of Evil, section Rebellion - Methodical, Deliberate, and Calculated.

> "God could hate evil and yet permit it in order to carry out an astounding, far-reaching redemptive plan in Christ, one that would forever overshadow the evil and sufferings of this present world." (Alcorn, p. 57) See chapter 8, Defeating Evil, for more information pertaining to the Lords's redemptive plan.

So does this mean God can never defeat evil without destroying free will? The answer, thankfully, is No. God had a plan before the beginning of time—before laying the foundations of the world. We know that God is all good and sovereign—and He certainly wants to defeat evil. And if God is supreme (omnipotent; omnipresent; omniscient), then certainly God must have a plan to destroy evil without destroying freedom, love, and mankind who is completely immersed in sin.

If there is not a way, then one must ask the question, why did God create mankind and allow so much terrible pain, suffering, and heartache throughout history based on an idea that would eventually fail? **God had a solution before creation—<u>a solution that Satan and his legion of rebellious angels could not foresee.</u>** This best possible solution is "*the defeat of evil without the destruction of freedom.*" (Geisler, p. 40)

Chapter 8

Defeating Evil

> *"He was despised and rejected by mankind, a man of suffering, and familiar with pain. Like one from whom people hide their faces he was despised, and we held him in low esteem. Surely he took up our pain and bore our suffering, yet we considered him punished by God, stricken by him, and afflicted."* — 1 Peter 1:18-19, NIV

God's Provision for Sin

Are you troubled and anxious by the amount of evil, suffering, depravity, and injustice in our world? It seems to go on and on unabated and to be ever increasing—men, women, and children suffering every kind of heinous, unimaginable physical evil; violence, immorality, depravity, and terrorism worldwide; dictatorial third world nations testing nuclear weapons and threatening nuclear war; and recent aggressive incursions into northern Israel by Russian and Iranian drones based in Syria. (Hal Lindsey, February 16, 2018) And the utterly incompetent withdrawal of the U.S. from Afghanistan on August 31, 2021, after a 20 year occupation (2001 - 2021) leaving many thousands of allies (Afghan interpreters, civilian Americans, and others) stranded and in great peril. Something is obviously wrong with the world. Mankind is bent on evil, and our world is suffering and groaning due to the consequences of sin. (For more information, see book, *Word in Denial - Defiant Nature of Mankind*.)

As a consequence of free will, God "anticipated sin and the suffering it would bring" and established a plan before the foundation of the world. See next section, Best Possible Solution.

As stated in chapter 7, God foreknew (before the foundation of the world) the problem with "free will," love, and evil. **The problem can be briefly restated as follows**: Without "free will" there is no love but "free will" also makes evil (sin) possible, and because God's nature is completely opposed to evil (sin) (Isaiah 6; Habakkuk 1:13), God had to find a way to eliminate evil without destroying free will, love, and mankind who is completely immersed in sin (immorality, depravity, violence, lawlessness, greed, and idolatry).

"God sovereignly created angels and human beings and gave them freedom to choose. He knew what choices angels and humans would make under what circumstances. While he could have intervened to stop them from sinning, he wanted them to choose freely, not under constraint. Furthermore, he planned to use the evil and suffering he foresaw to reveal himself in Christ and his redemptive plan." (Alcorn, p. 238)

"God is accomplishing his redemptive work in our lives...conquer evil and eliminate suffering [and pain] *'so that in the coming ages he might show the immeasurable riches of his grace in kindness toward us in Christ Jesus'*" (Ephesians 2:7, ESV). (Alcorn, p. 26)

"More than this, God's plan made provision for sin [of mankind] by means of the suffering [by the Cross] of the Son of God [Jesus Christ]." (Deffinbaugh, p. 6)

"Do we [you] think that God is harsh in allowing sin to enter the world to produce pain and suffering?" (Deffinbaugh, p. 6) But there was no other choice—either a world without love or a world with love and free will (freedom of choice) which opens the door to evil (sin), pain, and suffering, and eventual physical and spiritual death.

People ask why would a loving God create a world full of pain and suffering—but the real question is "**why would a loving God come into the world He created to suffer and die to pay for my sin?**" (Mitchell, p. 2) [Bold added] **God's plan was to eliminate evil without destroying free will and love and redeem a fallen mankind immersed in sin—but the plan required the Son of God (God incarnate) to become a sacrificial lamb for our sins.**

"The messianic text found in Isaiah 52:13-53:12 depicts the worst suffering any one person has ever endured. Remarkably, his suffering wasn't because of his own sin; it was for 'our' infirmities, 'our' sorrows, 'our' transgressions, 'our' iniquities." (Alcorn, p. 209) [Bold added]

> [14] "Many were **appalled at him...his appearance was so disfigured beyond that of any man...his form marred beyond human likeness...**[3] **He was despised and rejected** by men, **a man of sorrows, and familiar with suffering...**[4] **He took up our infirmities and carried our sorrows...we considered him stricken by God, smitten by him, and afflicted...**[5] **pierced for our transgressions...crushed for our iniquities...the punishment that brought us peace was upon him, and by his wounds we are healed...**[6] **the Lord has laid on him the iniquity of us all.** [7] **He was oppressed and afflicted,** yet **he did not open his mouth** [He remained silent]; he was **led like a lamb to the slaughter...**[10] **it was the Lords's will to crush him and cause him to suffer...the Lord makes his life a guilt offering...**[12] **For he bore the sin of many**" (Isaiah 52:13-53:12 (NIV). [Bold added]

> [23] "This man was handed over to you by God's deliberate plan and foreknowledge; and you, with the help of wicked men put him to death by nailing him to the cross. [24] But God raised him from the dead, freeing him from the agony of death, because it was impossible for death to keep its hold on him" (Acts 2:23-24, NIV).

> [18] "For you know that it was not with perishable things such as silver or gold that you were redeemed from the empty way of life handed down to you from your ancestors, [19] but with the precious blood of Christ, a lamb without blemish or defect. [20] **He was chosen before the creation of the world, but was revealed in these last times for your sake.** [21] Through him you believe in God, who raised him from the dead and glorified him, and so your faith and hope are in God" (1 Peter 1:18-21, NIV). [Bold added]

"He came in humiliation, many imagined Him conceived out of wedlock, a shameful thing in that era. He grew up in a town of ill repute: 'Nazareth! Can anything good come from there?' [John 1:46, NIV]...'He had no beauty or majesty to attract us to him, nothing in his appearance that we should desire him' (Isaiah 53:2, NIV). He worked as a humble carpenter...He lived in relative poverty...They called him a liar: 'No, he deceives the people' (John 7:12, NIV). Long before his crucifixion, he endured these indignities and much more." (Alcorn, p. 207)

"**On the cross Jesus suffered the worst pain in history**...The Cross is a mirror showing us the heart-stopping magnitude of our depravity and offers a terrible glimpse of Hell's misery...**The Cross is also a lens showing us**

> "We cannot imagine the depths of [physical and spiritual] agony He endured...He must suffer [He suffered] all the cruelties and humiliations that wicked men and the devil could devise. He must endure [He endured] the cross and its shame, taunts, spittle, and jeers; its nakedness, nails, struggling for breath, parching thirst, and looming, all but inescapable death." (Arnaud, p. 56-57)

God's uncompromising holiness and wrath that demand such a price for sin. It's also a magnifying glass showing us the **sweeping vastness of God's grace and love, that <u>he would be willing to pay a price he knew would be so horrific</u>.**" [Bold added] (Alcorn, p. 208)

"The temptation to end it all must have been overwhelming. With no more than a thought, just the unspoken word *'Come'*, Christ could have called upon waiting armies to strike down his torturers and bring him instant relief. <u>*Perhaps the greatest wonder is not that Jesus went to the cross but that he stayed on it...It's one thing to suffer terribly, another to choose to suffer terribly*</u>. Evil and suffering formed the crucible in which God demonstrated his love to mankind...God does not merely empathize with our sufferings. **He actually suffers. Jesus is God. What Jesus suffered, God suffered.**" [Bold and italics added] (Alcorn, p. 209)

Jesus said, *"I lay down my life for the sheep...No one takes if from me, but I lay it down of my own accord"* (John 10:15, 18, NIV). "In his love for us, God self-imposed the sentence of death on our behalf. One thing we must never say about God—that he doesn't understand what it means to be abandoned utterly, suffer terribly, and die miserably...In his haunting cry, *'Why have you forsaken me?'*

> "..Jesus suffered the same trials and temptations we do. God understands our worst losses and heartbreaks..."
> [Bold added] (Alcorn, p. 211, 213)

> God will deal with sin either by grace (mercy) or by wrath. John 3:36 (NIV) says, *"Whoever believes in the Son has eternal life, but whoever rejects the Son will not see life, for God's wrath remains on him."* Those who do not accept Jesus Christ as their Savior will remain under the Lord's wrath.

> People ask why would a loving God create a world full of pain and suffering—but the real question is "why would a loving God come into the world He created to suffer and die to pay for my sin?" Because God had a plan to preserve free will and love, destroy evil, and redeem fallen mankind—**but on one condition, mankind must freely accept God's free gift of pardon when Jesus carried the sins of humanity on the Cross**. [Bold added] (Mitchell, p. 2)
>
> "God allowed Jesus' temporary suffering so he could prevent our eternal suffering... Christ's atonement guarantees the final end of evil and suffering." (Alcorn p. 206-207)

Christ identifies with our despair [Psalm 22:1; Mark 15:34; Matthew 27:46]...So the Father turned away...the oneness within the Godhead knew separation...He cried out because any separation from his Father constituted an infinite horror..." (Alcorn, p. 214, 215)

Tim Keller explains,

"The physical pain was nothing compared to the spiritual experience of ...abandonment...Jesus Christ...knows first hand despair, rejection, loneliness, poverty, bereavement, torture, and imprisonment. **On the Cross he went beyond even the worst human suffering and experienced cosmic rejection and pain that exceeds ours as infinitely as his knowledge and power exceeds ours.**" [Bold added] (Keller, p. 30; as cited in Alcorn, 215)

> The two distinct natures of our Lord Jesus Christ are united as one person—total deity and total human. The Lord Jesus is equal to God the Father and God the Holy Spirit, yet different in that He is also a true man, yet sinless.

"...Jesus endured the punishment of Hell [and] when he said, *'It is finished,'* signaling he had paid the redemptive price, Jesus ceased to bear the penalty for our sin...The triune God had been restored to...complete oneness." (Alcorn, p. 215-216)

"God devised a way for His love (agape love, a sacrificial love) to deliver sinners from His wrath [death] while not compromising His righteousness and justice [love and free will]. Jesus Christ took upon Himself a human nature (God incarnate), lived as a true man, and never once sinned. He therefore qualified to voluntarily take upon Himself the penalty and punishment for our sins. He died in our place and secured a true forgiveness for each one who will receive it as a gift. Salvation cannot be given if any human merit is attached to it. Salvation is an absolute gift." (Hal Lindsey, December 30, 2016)

As Alcorn explains, "From the beginning, God planned that his Son [Jesus Christ] should deal the death blow to Satan, evil, and suffering, to reverse the Curse [see chapter 5], redeem a fallen humanity, and repair a broken world." (Alcorn, p. 51) *"The reason the Son of God appeared was to destroy the devil's work"* (1 John 3:8, NIV).

Why did Jesus have to be the sacrificial Lamb of God? Because of sin (rebellion) by the first man, Adam, against his Creator (Genesis 3:6; Romans 5:12), creation was cursed by God (Genesis 3:14-19)—in effect leading to a contaminated and corrupt world. All men are guilty of sin (Romans 3:23; 1 John 1:8, 10) and sin always carries a death sentence, *"For the wages of sin is death, but the gift of God is eternal life in Christ Jesus our Lord"* (Romans 6:23, NIV).

> "God could hate evil and yet permit it in order to carry out an astounding, far-reaching redemptive plan in Christ, one that would forever overshadow the evil and sufferings of this present world." (Alcorn, p. 57)

Only Jesus, the Son of God, could be the Mediator between God the Father and desperately sinful mankind, and without Jesus, there would be no reconciliation and no redemption (salvation; restoration) for humanity. The complexity of the concept of the God-Man in Jesus Christ is especially difficult to comprehend, but it was necessary to redeem creation lost to sin. God loved us so much that He sent His Son Jesus to take our place and become our "redeemer." (Hal Lindsey, March 20, 2015; March 27, 2015; September 4, 2015)

The "curse of death pronounced on Adam is God's means for our cure" through the life, death, and resurrection of Jesus Christ— **He preserved free will and love, destroyed evil, and redeemed fallen mankind with the condition that mankind must accept God's free gift of pardon that Jesus purchased when He suffered the sins of humanity on the Cross**. It is the death and resurrection of our Lord Jesus Christ, on our behalf, which saves us from our sins and provides us with the promise of eternal life. Jesus accepted our iniquities and in turn gave us His godliness. (Deffinbaugh, p. 6)

Unlike Adam and Eve we were born into sin and are doomed to die. But like Adam and Eve, we have "free will" to choose for or against God—**to obey God and accept the gift of pardon or live a life of disobedience and face God's wrath and eternal separation.** "We may either cling to our identification with Adam (our sin nature) and die, or we may be given a new identity in Jesus Christ, and live." (Deffinbaugh, p. 9)

Best Possible Solution

In His grace, mercy, and loving-kindness, God was able to preserve "free will" (and love) and defeat evil by sending His Son to die on the cross and take (suffer, endure) the penalty of our sin (offer atonement for the sins of humanity), reconciling us to God the Father and making eternal life with Him possible. This is the best possible plan:

1) *"God is love"* (1 John 4:8, 4:16, NIV). The word "love" is translated 'agape love' found only in humans and God (Romans 5:8)—an unconditional, self-sacrificing love. God allowed "free will" because without freedom there is no love and fellowship with God (there is no love without freedom).

2) Free will (freedom of choice) gives people the freedom to choose for or against God; and many people in this world will 'harden their hearts' (Mark 8:17-18; Ephesians 4:18; cf. Luke 8:8:10-12; Matthew 13:14) and choose against God no matter what the rationale—there will always be people who will choose evil (sin) over love and goodness. It is undeniable that freedom is good but freedom makes evil possible.

3) **Sin leads to pain and suffering, disease, and eventual death, or the Curse**—*"...the wages of sin is death, but the gift of God is eternal life in Christ Jesus our Lord"* (Romans 6:23, NIV).

4) Jesus Christ bore the penalty of our sins on the Cross, reconciling us (reuniting; restoring harmony) with God the Father.

5) Each person must either accept or reject this "free gift" of pardon while on earth— **earth is the 'testing ground.'** Then at the Great White Throne Judgment (Revelation 20:11-13), people will be separated according to their "free will" choice while on earth (Matthew 13:30, 25:32-34; 2 Thessalonians 1:8-9). For more information, see Appendix C.

6) Heaven will remain sinless. It will not be possible to sin in heaven among the redeemed—those who have accepted the free gift of pardon from our Lord Jesus Christ. **"Free will" (freedom) will have been fulfilled during our life on earth** (1 Corinthians 13:12; Revelation 21:1-5; Ephesians 1:4; 2 Timothy 1:9-10).

Those redeemed and in heaven will have **already made the "free will" choice for God and accepted the free gift of pardon while on earth,** and through the process of life on earth suffered and died as Jesus. In Hebrews 9:22, NIV, *"In fact, the law requires that nearly everything be cleansed with blood, and without the shedding of blood there is no forgiveness."* As described in Hebrews 2:14-18, the death of Jesus Christ on the cross and his resurrection brought reconciliation (restored harmony) between God and mankind.

The question of preserving free will and a sinless heaven **must be settled before heaven.** Otherwise, if people are given free will in heaven, "what is the guarantee that sin will not break out again?" (See chapter 4, The Origin of Sin.) Sin in heaven must be impossible because heaven is described as 'perfect' (1 Corinthians 13:10, 12) and sinless (1 John 3:2; Revelation 21:4, 22:3). (Geisler, p. 62)

According to the Bible a final victory over evil will involve the banishment of physical and moral evil and freedom from sin in heaven:

"physical evils will be banished (Romans 8:18-21; Revelation 21:1-4); moral evils will be separated and quarantined so they can no longer spread (Matthew 25:31-46; Revelation 20:11-15)." (Geisler, p. 44)

Summary of Alternatives

1) If God does not allow "free will" (no freedom of choice) while on earth → there would be no sin, but there would be no love or fellowship with our Creator; people would be robots (machines) forced to honor God without love.

2) If God allows "free will" (freedom to choose to obey or disobey God) while on earth → sin would be permitted and defeated through the sacrifice of Jesus Christ on the Cross; "free will" would be "fulfilled" during our lifetime on earth (**earth is the testing ground**); and love would be preserved; and goodness and mercy would be attained by the greatest number of people.

> Many people will turn away from God and others will not → without destroying "free will," sin (evil) will be allowed to enter the world through people who **defiantly** choose to turn away from God → *"...the wages of sin is death..."* Romans 6:23, James 1:15 → **Jesus Christ endured the sins of humanity on the Cross and those who accept the free gift of pardon offered by Jesus Christ, Son of God, will be saved** from eternal spiritual death and their destiny is a sinless heaven (**"free will" will have been "fulfilled" on earth, love preserved, and evil defeated**) → but sadly for those who turn away from God, their destiny is hell—eternal separation from God.

The purpose of Jesus dying on the Cross for our sins (as a **sacrificial lamb bearing the sins of humanity and offering a free gift of pardon to all mankind) was to preserve freedom and love, rid the universe of evil forever, and start a divine family in His image in Heaven.** The Cross assures the defeat of Satan and evil. *"The reason the Son of God appeared was to destroy the devil's work"* (1 John 3:8, NIV). Through the Cross, *"He disarmed the rulers [fallen angels] and authorities and put them to open shame, by triumphing over them"* (Colossians 2:15, ESV).

"He [God] foresaw that every world of free creatures He could ever make would have some who would freely choose to sin. So while such a world is *conceivable*, God knew it was *unachievable*." (Geisler, p. 64-65)

A God of love cannot force people to love Him—to love goodness. Otherwise people would be created as robots. God can only gently persuade. It would certainly be best if everyone understood the consequences of turning away from God and are eventually saved, but as we can see in today's world and throughout the history of mankind, this is not the case.

Planet Earth
God's Testing Ground

God gives us choices to test us, like Abraham and Isaac in Genesis 22:12; and like the Jewish people following God's instructions during the exodus from Egypt in Exodus 16:4.

Free will is a good thing; there is no love without freedom, but "free will" makes evil possible. With "free will" could evil have been avoided? Unfortunately, the answer is No. There are always people who will 'harden their hearts' and choose evil (sin). The only way God could destroy evil is to destroy "free will," and the consequences of destroying "free will" would be to destroy the possibility to love—there is no love without freedom.

God chose the best world possible—a world of "free will" where love is preserved and sin is tried (even with ensuing pain, suffering, decay, disease, and death) and defeated rather than a world where there is no free will, no love, and no sin. Man's purpose is to be part of the Kingdom and family of God, but we can only reach this destiny through a process of trials of this world—<u>a testing ground to either accept or reject the free gift of pardon through Jesus Christ. This is why we are living our lives on earth</u>.

> In the Book of Revelation, God says, *"He who overcomes [perseveres through the sin and temptations of this life] shall inherit all things, and I will be his God and he shall be My son"* (Revelation 21:7).
>
> Again, the wording reaffirms shared rule with God over all creation as His children. **Man's purpose is to be part of the Kingdom and family of God—but we can only reach this destiny through the trials of this world and by accepting the free gift of pardon through Jesus Christ.**

> *"We rejoice in our sufferings, because we know that suffering produces perseverance; perseverance, character; and character, hope"* (Romans 5:3-4, NIV).

People who die and go to heaven (whose names are written in Book of Life) made the choice for God while they were still on earth. Earth is the testing ground as predetermined by God before creation (Ephesians 1:4; 2 Timothy 1:9-10; 1 Corinthians 13:12; Revelation 21:1-5)—before laying the foundation of the world.

As stated in the previous section, "the Bible describes heaven as 'perfect' (1 Corinthians 13:10, 12) and sinless (1 John 3:2; Revelation 21:4; 22:3). The only real guarantee that heaven will remain sinless forever is that it will no longer be possible to sin." Otherwise, if given a choice, there will always be some people who will choose to sin. (Geisler, p. 62)

Man is given time here on earth to experience life, repent of sins, and make a "free will" choice for or against God by accepting or rejecting the free gift of pardon offered by the Son of God. <u>"Free will" will have been fulfilled during our life on earth</u> (1 Corinthians 13:12; Revelation 21:1-5; Ephesians 1:4; 2 Timothy 1:9-10).

> People are allowed "free will" on earth in order to make a choice, and then in heaven a person will no longer be able to sin. **The time here on earth is the "free will" testing ground for humans.**

epilogue

evil still exists in our world

Today, about 6,000 years after creation and 1,985 years after the crucifixion and resurrection of Jesus, we know that evil still exists and permeates the fabric of our society and human life—and it seems to be worse than ever. Crime, immorality, arrogance, violence, lawlessness, and indifference, and threats of nuclear war by third world nations seem to be commonplace. It is obvious that evil is not yet defeated but seems only to grow worse in the hearts of mankind. It is certainly much worse today than it was 30 years ago. When will God bring an end to the evil in today's world?

> The end of the "testing period" is closer than people might think. We are in the "last days"—yet many in the world have no clue what is going on as it relates to Bible prophecy. What can we expect in the near future? The answer is detailed in chapters 8 through 12 in the book, *World in Denial - Defiant Nature of Mankind – Biblical Account (Prophetic Evidence for a Divine Creator)*.

Through Jesus Christ's suffering and death on the cross for the sins of the world, God has already defeated evil without destroying our freedom and love. As Randy Alcorn explains, "From the beginning, God planned that his Son [Jesus Christ] should deal the death blow to Satan, evil, and suffering, to reverse the Curse [see chapter 8], redeem a fallen humanity, and repair a broken world." *"The reason the Son of God appeared was to destroy the devil's work"* (1 John 3:8, NIV). (Alcorn, p. 51)

Inconceivably, many people in this world will remain defiant to the end of their lives—they turn away from God the Father and His Son, the Lord Jesus Christ, and fully embrace sin and false gods. Many have "hardened their hearts" (Ephesians 4:18) and do not want to be saved. They remain apathetic—indifferent, uninterested, unbelieving, and uncaring. God wants to save all, but not all want to be saved. *"Anyone who chooses to be a friend of the world becomes an enemy of God"* (James 4:4, NIV).

> God foreknew that a free world where all mankind would be saved is conceivable but not achievable. A God of love cannot force people to love Him—to love goodness. Otherwise people would be created as robots. God can only gently persuade. It would certainly be best if everyone understood the consequences of turning away from God and are eventually saved, but as we can see in today's world and throughout the history of mankind, this is not the case.

The nature of an all-good God assures us that this world, which He created, is the best world possible without violating "free will"—the freedom to choose between good and evil. No other possible world is morally superior where people are given the freedom to choose between good and evil; where sin is permitted and defeated; where "free will" has been "fulfilled" during our lifetime on earth and love is preserved; where goodness and mercy are attained by the greatest number of people; and where we are guaranteed a sinless heaven without violating freedom of choice.

God wants everyone to be saved. *"For God so loved the world [not just select individuals] that He gave His only begotten Son, that whosoever believeth in Him should not perish but have everlasting life"* (John 3:16, KJV). Indeed, *"God our Savior...desires all people to be saved and to come to the knowledge of the truth"* (1 Timothy 2:3-4 ESV) for *"The Lord is...patient with you and not wanting anyone to perish, but everyone to come to repentance"* (2 Peter 3:9).

No one can force another to "freely" believe in God—"forcing people to freely believe is a contradiction in terms." (Geisler, p. 67) God is love (1 John 4:16), and love can only work persuasively. A God of love cannot force people to love Him—to love goodness and holiness. Even Jesus was unable to persuade all His people (Jews) to believe (Matthew 23:37). At the end of this life on earth, there are just two kinds of people: those who believe in the saving grace of Jesus Christ and those who do not.

> Allowing physical evil to exist (for a short time, relatively speaking) in a free world is the best possible way to produce the best possible world. Our own secular society is an illustration of this point. We permit cars and boats knowing there will be occasional accidents. Nonetheless, we deem that human freedom, love, and happiness justify permitting the physical evils that may take place.
>
> "God is not producing or promoting [an] evil means to attain a good end. He is permitting them." Parents permit a possible accident when they let their teenager drive the family car, or participate in sports such as football, basketball or baseball, but parents are not promoting an accident. (Geisler, p. 69)

Paul speaks of the on-going effects of Adam's sin and the ultimate cure in Romans 5:12-21 and 1 Corinthians 15:20-22. (Deffinbaugh, p. 5)

> *"Therefore, just as sin entered the world through one man, and death through sin, and in this way death came to all men, because all sinned"* (Romans 5:12-13, NIV).
>
> *"For just as through the disobedience of the one man [Adam] the many were made sinners, so also through the obedience of the one man [Jesus] the many will be made righteous"* (Romans 5:19, NIV).
>
> *"But now Christ has been raised from the dead, the first fruits of those who are asleep. For since by a man [Adam] came death, by a man [Jesus] also came the resurrection of the dead. For as in Adam all die, so also in Christ all shall be made alive"* (1 Corinthians 15:20-22, NIV).

Those who choose for God and accept the free gift of pardon will inherit from God "all things"—joint ownership and rule over not just the earth but the entire universe and spirit realm. This most incredible part of mankind's destiny was foretold in the Old Testament by Moses when he stated that *"...the sun, the moon, and the stars, all the host of heaven ... the Lord your God has given to all the peoples under the whole heaven as a heritage"* (Deuteronomy 4:19, NKJV).

> As previously stated, the end of the story is closer than most people realize. What we can expect in the near future is detailed in chapters 8 through 12 in the book, *World in Denial - Defiant Nature of Mankind – Biblical Account (Prophetic Evidence for a Divine Creator)*.

making the right choice

Our eternal destiny is either heaven or hell (separation from God)—eternal and everlasting. For those who have turned their back on God—stop and seriously reconsider the consequences of your decision and motivation. Eternal life in the Kingdom of Heaven is freely offered during your time here on earth through our Lord Jesus Christ, the Messiah, who is *"King of Kings and Lord of Lords"* (Revelation 19:16, NIV). And according to Romans 9:5, Jesus is God in the fullest sense.

Jesus shed His blood, suffered, and died on the Cross to save us from our sins and the wrath of God—from the eternal loneliness, darkness, and torment of hell—but only if we accept the gift of pardon through faith and repentance of sins. The Bible tells us that Heaven is available to everyone—it doesn't matter who you are, how old you are, where you live, or what sins you may have committed. That is why Jesus is called Savior. He graciously offers life in Heaven (Paradise)—but there is **only one way** and it is through Jesus Christ—**not multiple ways** as some suggest who believe in the same God for all religions (COEXIST bumper stickers). We have to sincerely repent of our sins and accept the gift of pardon by faith.

In our present state, man is sinful and separated from God; Jesus Christ is God's only provision for man's sin; we must individually receive Jesus Christ as Savior and Lord; and we cannot 'earn' our way into Heaven by our 'good deeds.'

> *"For it is by grace you have been saved, through faith—and this not from yourselves, it is the gift of God—not by works, so that no one can boast"* (Ephesians 2:8-9, NIV).

> *"He who believes in Him is not judged; he who does not believe is judged already, because he has not believed in the name of the only begotten Son of God"* (John 3:18, NIV).

> *"For God so loved the world that he gave his only begotten Son, that whosoever believeth in Him should not perish but have everlasting life"* (John 3:16, KJV).

> *"I am the good shepherd. The good shepherd lays down his life for the sheep"* (John 10:11, NIV).

> *"Do not let your hearts be troubled. You believe in God; believe also in me. My Father's house has many rooms [mansions; abiding places]; if that were not so, would I have told you that I am going there to prepare a place for you? And if I go and prepare a place for you, I will come back and take you to be with me that you also may be where I am [in Heaven]. You know the way to the place where I am going"* (John 14:1-4, NIV).

The only unpardonable sin is to reject the free gift of pardon offered by Jesus Christ, the promised Messiah...who stepped out of Eternity (*"His goings forth are from long ago, from the days of eternity,"* Micah 5:2, NAS) and became a guilt offering. He became a sacrificial 'Lamb of God' on the Cross—the ultimate and final sin offering for Israel and the whole world...and bore our iniquities so we can be cleansed of all our sins. He took the penalty for our sins upon Himself—**but we have to believe it, accept it, and receive it in our hearts by faith.**

> "Life on Earth is a dot, a brief window of opportunity; life in Heaven (and ultimately on the New Earth) is a line going out from that dot for eternity. If we're smart, we'll live not for the dot but for the line." (Alcorn, 2017, p. 1)

Invite Him into your life as Lord and Savior, believe He died on the Cross for all your sins, and rose from the grave. There will be no peace in our heart until we make peace with God through His Son Jesus Christ, the promised Messiah, who died for us so we might have life after death in Heaven. Consider the following principles: (Pratte, p. 1)

> All men are guilty of sin and need forgiveness - Romans 3:23, 6:23; 1 John 1:8, 10.
>
> God desires to have all men turn from sin and be saved - 1 Timothy 2:4; 2 Peter 3:9; Titus 2:11, 12.
>
> Jesus died to make salvation available to all men - 1 Timothy 2:6; Hebrews. 2:9; John 3:16; Matthew 11:28-30.
>
> To be saved, men must hear, believe, and obey the gospel - John 6:44-45, 8:24, 32; Hebrews 5:9; 2 Thessalonians 1:8-9; 1 Peter 1:22; Romans 1:16, 6:17-18, 10:14, 17.
>
> God desires for all men to learn the gospel so they have the opportunity to believe and obey - 1 Timothy 2:4; Matthew 28:18-20; Mark 16:15-16; Luke 24:47; Acts 2:29, 38, 17:30-31; Colossians 1:28.
>
> The gospel offers all that is good and all that we need to please God - John 14:26, 16:13; 2 Peter 1:3; 2 Timothy 3:16- 17; Acts 20:20, 27; Matthew 28:18-20; James 1:25.

All people need the gospel, God wants all people to have the gospel, and so the gospel was completely and accurately revealed in the first century to the apostles. The Gospel of Jesus Christ has remained available throughout history, and it is available to all people worldwide through missionary outreach and advanced communications in television, radio, and the internet.

God is long suffering: *"The Lord is not slow in keeping his promise, as some understand slowness. Instead he is patient with you, not wanting anyone to perish, but everyone to come to repentance"* (2 Peter 3:9, NIV). We thank God that He loves us enough to provide a way for us to escape the judgment for our sins. By accepting Jesus Christ as our Lord and Savior, and by the grace of God, we are granted forgiveness of sins, mercy, and salvation with the promise of everlasting life (John 3:16; Ephesians 2:8-9).

In their book, *Charting the End Times*, Drs. Tim LaHaye and Thomas Ice describe The Way to Paradise: (LaHaye and Ice, p. 133-134)

> "... those who go to Paradise and those who end up in Hades are sinners. The latter die in their sins, while those who reside in Paradise were forgiven of their sins sometime during their life [on earth]. Jesus Himself gave us clear directions on how to obtain admittance to this glorious place when He said, *'I am the way, and the truth, and the life; no one comes to the Father but through Me'* (John 14:6, NIV). Only through Jesus Christ can we gain access to the Father, who is in heaven (where Paradise is now located). The Bible says that all men deserve to go to hell (Romans 3:23, 6:23), and only through faith in the Lord Jesus Christ and His finished work on the cross can we escape Hades and hell. John 1:12 says, *'As many as received Him, to them He gave the right to become children of God, even to those who believe in His name.'*"

"To activate the eternal effects of God's forgiveness of sins through the death of His Son, **a person must call on the name of the Lord and be saved** (Romans 10:13). There is no other way—and no second chance." [Bold added]

This final passage is borrowed from the Introduction to the Book of Psalms, The NIV Study Bible [which should be read by all]:

"Under God creation is a cosmos—an orderly and systematic whole. What we distinguish as 'nature' and history had for them one Lord, under whose rule all things worked together. Through the creation the Great King's majestic glory is displayed. He is good (wise, righteous, faithful, amazingly benevolent and merciful—evoking trust), and he is great (his knowledge, thoughts and works are beyond human comprehension—evoking reverent awe). By his good and lordly rule he is shown to be the Holy One."

"As The Great King by right of creation and enduring absolute sovereignty, he ultimately will not tolerate any worldly power that opposes or denies or ignores him. He will come to rule the nations so that all will be compelled to acknowledge him. This expectation is no doubt the root and broadest scope of the psalmists' long view of the future. Because the Lord is the Great King beyond all challenge, his righteous and peaceable kingdom will come, overwhelming all opposition and purging the creation of all rebellion against his rule—such will be the ultimate outcome of history."

"As the Great King on whom all creatures depend, he opposes the "proud," those who rely on their own resources (and/or the gods they have contrived) to work out their own destiny. These are the ones who ruthlessly wield whatever power they possess to attain worldly wealth, status and security; who are a law to themselves and exploit others as they will. In the Psalter, **this kind of "pride" is the root of all evil**. Those who embrace it, though they seem to prosper, will be brought down to death, their final end. The "humble," the "poor and needy," those who acknowledge their dependence on the Lord in all things—these are the ones that God delights." [Bold and underline added]

God will deal with sin either by grace or by wrath. John 3:36 (NIV) says, *"Whoever believes in the Son has eternal life, but whoever rejects the Son will not see life, for God's wrath remains on him."* Those who do not accept Jesus Christ as their Savior will remain under the Lord's wrath.

It's not too late to choose eternal life. **All that is required is acceptance of God's free gift of pardon through faith and repentance of sin**. There is nothing you can do to earn grace [mercy]; Jesus has paid the price for you (Romans 3:24).

If what you see happening in the world makes you fearful or anxious, don't be. If you accept this free gift of pardon, you will inherit eternal life and won't be here during the seven year tribulation. (For more information re the tribulation period, see chapters 11 and 12 in the book, *World in Denial - Defiant Nature of Mankind (Prophetic Evidence for a Divine Creator)*.

God is holy, righteous, and merciful and through our Lord Jesus Christ offers the gift of eternal salvation (John 3:16, 5:24, 14:6; Romans 10:9, 13). *"For it is by grace you have been saved through faith..."* (Ephesians 2:8, NIV).

People lest not forget the Lord is **omnipresent, omnipotent, and omniscient** (Romans 8:29; Ephesians 1:4-5; 1 Corinthians 2:7); **He is inside and outside the universe;** and "**the Lord is a warrior**" (Exodus 15:3, NIV)—"**He does whatever pleases Him**" (Psalms 115:3, 135:6; Job 23:13; Daniel 4:35, NIV), and **"He is to be feared"** (1 Chronicles 16:25; Psalm 96:4; Isaiah 8:13; Job 25:15-16, NIV). **But most importantly,** *"God is love"* (1 John 4:8, 4:16, NIV). (See chapter 1, Who is God?)

Appendix A
Why Didn't God Make Us Like Angels?

God reveals that He created mankind (male and female) in His own image and likeness (Genesis 1:26-27)—language that **indicates offspring or children of God** (Genesis 5:1-3).

> [26]"Then God said, '**Let us make man in our image**, according to our likeness; and let them rule over the fish of the sea and over the birds of the sky and over the cattle and over all the earth, and over every creeping thing that creeps on the earth.'"
>
> [27]"And God created man in His own image, **in the image of God He created him; male and female He created them**" (Genesis 1:26-27, NAS). [Bold added]

Man was made in the likeness of God for His glory. The reason for our existence is to become a member of the family of God—His family (1 John 3:2; Romans 8:16-17). Every human being living today has the "free will' opportunity to become a member of that divine eternal family. In obedience to God the Father, **humans will be allowed to share God's divine existence forever as children of God and rule over creation with Him (Genesis 1:28)**. For more information, see chapter 3, sections Creation and Purpose of Mankind and What is the Image of God?

People who die and go to heaven (whose names are written in the Book of Life) made the choice for God while they were still on earth. **Earth is the testing ground** as predetermined by God before creation (Ephesians 1:4; 2 Timothy 1:9-10; 1 Corinthians 13:12; Revelation 21:1-5)—before laying the foundation of the world.

"The Bible describes heaven as 'perfect' (1 Corinthians 13:10, 12) and sinless (1 John 3:2; Revelation 21:4, 22:3); and the only real guarantee that heaven will remain sinless forever is that it will no longer be possible to sin."

There is **no Scripture describing angels created in the image of God** (although omission of Scripture does not imply angels were not created in God's image). Angels have a different function or role than mankind as described in chapter 2. **Angels are all ministering (pure) immortal celestial spirits (Hebrews 1:14; Luke 20:35-36, 24:39) who were created to represent God and to defend His interests (Psalm 148:5-60)**; and they praise the Lord because He created them and made them secure in the created universe.

As an angel, it would be almost impossible to turn away from God. The love of God by angels is too great. Angels were created with great intellect, wisdom, holiness, and understanding. Turning away from God would have been equivalent to humans voluntarily jumping into a fiery furnace—humans would never consider such an idea, and angels would never consider turning away from God. Logically, one would never consider turning against someone you truly love.

Once an angel "chooses against" God (Revelation 12:3-4), the decision can never be changed—there is no redemption. They are condemned forever with no prospect of redemption—*"God did not spare angels when they sinned, but sent them to hell..."* (2 Peter 2:4).

It was as final as a human's final choice during lifetime on earth (accepting the free gift of pardon or not; deciding for or against God) at the time of death (Hebrews 9:27). This is the reason God does not call on rebellious angels to repent or ask for forgiveness as He does with people (Acts 17:30). Angels fell by a total act of **pride** (1 Timothy 3:6; see chapter 4), and their decision against God is permanent.

Christ did not die for angels: *"...For surely it is not the angels that he helps, but he helps the offspring of Abraham"* (Hebrews 2:14-16, ESV).

Alcorn, R. (2009). *If God is Good.* Colorado Springs, CO: Multnomah Books, 47-54.

Geisler, N.L. (2011). *If God, Why Evil?* Minneapolis, MN: Bethany House Publishers, 92-93.

Appendix B
Issues of Pain and Suffering

All evil in today's world traces back to Adam disobeying God. Adam's free choice to disobey God resulted in separation from God—hence, decay and deterioration, pain and suffering, and disease and death. During the course of early history, man was given the individual and moral responsibility to pursue goodness and virtue and turn away from evil—but ultimately, man was consumed continually with wickedness and violence.

Eventually God gave man the Moral Code (the Ten Commandments; Exodus 20). All pain, suffering, and disease in the world is the result of the consequences of sin (moral evil)—decay and degradation resulting in mutational load and genetic burden as described in chapters 2 and 3 in the book, *evolution - The Greatest Deception in Modern History (Scientific Evidence for Divine Creation)*.

Evil is sin or iniquity; or choosing not to obey God. The consequences of evil are pain, suffering, decay (deterioration), disease, and death.

Moral evil is disobeying God—it is breaking the moral law (see Appendix D, section, The Moral Law), or any one of the Ten Commandments, or a departure from goodness.

Physical evil is immorality, lawlessness, violence, depravity, corruption, and persecution with its ensuing pain, suffering, decay, disease, and death. Physical evil is the result of moral evil in some way (disobeying God; the Moral Law).

As stated in chapter 5, section Immediate Effects of the Fall: Before sin entered the world, the world was good (Genesis 1:31). God "upheld" and continuously restored everything in the beginning (Colossians 1:17 and Hebrews 1:3), but when sin entered the world (through the first man, Adam—Genesis 3:6), God cursed the world (Genesis 3:14-19), God withdrew His blessings, and the perfect world began to degenerate—that is, suffer death and decay (Romans 5:12, 6:23, 8:22; James 1:15; 1 Corinthians 11:28-30).

The dominion of man (male and female) over the entire world (Genesis 1:26-28, 5:1-2) meant that when Adam sinned, all of creation was cursed as well.

The degeneration and dying process started slowly because of zero mutational load with Adam and Eve. Cain was the firstborn to Adam and Eve and would have received perfect genes from his parents because the effects of sin and the Curse were nonexistent in the beginning. Mutational load (genetic burden) is the cause of most, if not all diseases today.

An easy to understand explanation about the First and Second Laws of Thermodynamics and the cause of disease we see in today's world is found in chapters 2 and 3 in the book by Roger Gallop, *evolution - The Greatest Deception in Modern History (Scientific Evidence for Divine Creation)*.

> Physical evil in the world is the result of the fall of mankind. All physical evil with its ensuing pain, suffering, decay, disease, and death is directly or indirectly related to moral evil and free choice. According to many theology scholars, **moral evil accounts for all physical evils** (except the evils inflicted by Satan and other fallen angels or demons).

Physical evils are related, directly or indirectly, to free will choices of individuals: (Geisler, p. 73-77)

1. Directly self-inflicted: smoking, drinking alcohol, use of non-prescription drugs such as marijuana, cocaine, and heroin; auto accidents caused by DUI; eating the wrong foods; over-eating; and lack of exercise.

2. Indirectly self-inflicted: laziness; neglect of oneself, children, and the elderly; bad life-style choices (in conflict with the moral code); and indifference to the plight of others in the U.S. and worldwide.

3. Directly inflicted by other people: crime and violence; war and terrorism; physical or sexual abuse by parents or an authority figure (e.g., boss at work); auto accidents caused by DUI or texting while driving; and the list goes on.

4. Indirectly inflicted by other people: thoughtless choices (e.g., 'cutting corners' and 'greed' by corporate executives) resulting in job loss, ground and surface water pollution by industry, city, state and federal government, and air pollution by industry affecting the health of others, etc.

5. Indirectly inflicted (accidents) during normal lifestyle events: accidents during sports or recreational activities; drowning while swimming or water skiing; boating accidents; bicycling; unintentional recreational shooting deaths; mountain climbing or hiking accidents; amateur and professional team or individual sports, etc.

6. Physical evil may be connected to evil spirits (demons as often dramatized in Hollywood movies). God created only good creatures (Genesis 1:31; 1 Timothy 4:4), but some of them, led by Lucifer, a Cherub angel (who became Satan), rebelled against God (Revelation 12:4) and became evil spirits or demons.

According to the Bible, these evil spirits are opposed to God and God's people, and some sickness and suffering are attributed to demon possession (Matthew 9:32-33, 8:16, 15:22).

> "But I wonder how many times God has spared us from...tragedies without our knowing it? If God saved us from death fives times a day, how would we know? How many close calls do we have that we don't recognize, and how many never happen because God intervenes?"
> (Alcorn, p. 273)

Whether God has intervened to stop some physical evils, the answer is yes, and there are numerous examples inside and outside the Bible to demonstrate such miracles. **As to why He does not do it more often, especially for the very young and innocent, only God who is omniscient (all-knowing) knows the answer.**

> "...our present sufferings are not worth comparing with the glory that will be revealed in us" (Romans 8:18, NIV), and "For our light and momentary troubles are achieving for us an eternal glory that far out weighs them all" (2 Corinthians 4:17, NIV).

> "Oh the depth of the riches both of the wisdom and knowledge of God! How unsearchable are His judgments and unfathomable His ways, what might seem too much or too long!" (Romans 11:33, NAS)

> "The secret things belong to the LORD our God, but the things revealed belong to us and to our children forever, that we may follow all the words of this law" (Deuteronomy 29:29, NIV).

Physical disasters may be inflicted by God as a result of His justice (judgment) in punishing evil nations; for example, the defeat of the Canaanites by Joshua and the Jewish people (Exodus 23:27-29); plagues (Exodus chapters 7 through 11); famines (Isaiah 14:30); illnesses (2 Kings 20); and death (Romans 5:12; 1 Corinthians 11:28-30).

Why did God allow evil empires such as the Assyrian Empire (721 BC), Babylonian Empire (586 BC), and the Roman Empire (AD 70) to execute punishment (Habakkuk 1:12) on a people (the Jews) more righteous than themselves? This question is addressed in the epilogue (question #17) of the book by Roger Gallop, *World in Denial - Defiant Nature of Mankind (Prophetic Evidence for a Divine Creator)*.

> "God could hate evil and yet permit it in order to carry out an astounding, far-reaching redemptive plan in Christ, one that would forever overshadow the evil and sufferings of this present world." (Alcorn, p. 57) See chapter 8 for more info.

> "We rejoice in our sufferings, because we know that suffering produces perseverance; perseverance, character; and character, hope" (Romans 5:3-4, NIV).

We must understand that God of the Bible is sovereign and "governs all nations, bringing them into being (Amos 9:7, NIV) and calling them into account (Amos 1:3-2:3). He also uses one against another to carry out his purposes (Amos 6:14). He is the Great King who rules the whole universe (Amos 4:13, 5:8, 9:5-6). Because He is all-sovereign, the God of Israel holds the history and destiny of all peoples and the world in His hands. ...He is Lord over all." (NIV Study Bible (1985), Passage taken from the introduction to the Book of Amos)

The world today is moving away from the Bible and toward an increase of arrogance, immorality, depravity, corruption, lawlessness, and violence—a period described in Scripture as the Last Days (similar to the Antediluvian days as described in chapter 6). How do we know?

Fulfillment of super signs: 1) miraculous rebirth of the State of Israel in 1948; 2) repossession of the City of Jerusalem in 1967; 3) State of Israel surrounded by hostile Arab nations; 4) increase in arrogance, immorality, violence, lawlessness, terrorism, and greed (with no normal sense of right or wrong); 5) rise of Russia and its alliance with certain Muslim states such as Iran, Syria, and Turkey; 6) rise of China militarily and economically; and 7) increase in modern transportation and knowledge (supercomputers)—all prophesied in Scripture. See chapter 8 in the book, *World in Denial – Defiant Nature of Mankind (Prophetic Evidence for a Divine Creator)*.

Physical calamity is coming upon the world because most of the world is in denial of the Savior, Jesus Christ. Yet, there is a deep knowing in the human psyche, **a realization that something is not right with the world**. To the average American it is obvious that something is **WRONG**—what I refer to as the "gray veil." Romans 8:22 (NIV) states *"the whole creation groans and labors with **birth pangs**...."* [Bold added] Many believe the world is going through something akin to childbirth. That means that the **labor pangs are growing in frequency and intensity as we move toward a specific event.**

The *"whole Creation groans and labors..."* God has been long-suffering and tolerant in his judgment of the U.S. and the world, but the time is coming that the *"measure of sin is now full."* (See Genesis 15:16.) We are very close to the 'tipping point' of the seven year tribulation but the world seems oblivious to the reality of such events, *"though seeing, they may not see; though hearing, they may not understand"* (Luke 8:10-12, NIV).

> **Last days** (also called end times, end of time, end of days, final days)—is a time period (described in eschatology; or study of Bible prophecy) just prior to and including the seven year tribulation period preceding the Second Coming of Christ. In Judaism, the term "end of days" refers to the Messianic Age that includes an in-gathering of the Diaspora (exiled Jewish people) and the coming of the Messiah.

Allowing evil, hence pain and suffering, "was a necessary price to achieve a far greater eternal result." (Alcorn, p. 41-42) *"Our light and momentary troubles are achieving for us an eternal glory that far outweighs them all"* (2 Corinthians 4:17).

Bible Scripture
In Times of Pain and Suffering

In this life we all face the reality of pain, suffering, heartache, disease, and death as the direct result of sin. See chapter 5, Immediate Effects of the Fall, and beginning of this appendix.

We are in the last days ("end times") as described in chapters 6 - 12 of the book, *World in Denial - Defiant Nature of Mankind,* and we face the reality of an alarming increase of worldwide violence, terrorism, lawlessness, greed, immorality, and sexual depravity (including child trafficking and demonic sexual molestation of children by Catholic clergy and other deviant individuals). Also, most countries including the U.S. are facing the disappearance of the Moral Code (the Ten Commandments) which has led to the moral decline of public schools and universities.

We all feel the increase in anger, lies, lunacy and sick humor; persecution of Jews and Christians; lewdness, evil, and demonic themes beyond description on television and in Hollywood movies; routinely using the Lord's name in vain (blasphemy of the Holy Spirit; Mark 3:28-30; Exodus 20:7); constantly using sexually explicit language; distorted or false news in the main stream media; and the seemingly increase of worldwide bizarre weather patterns (including wildfires, flash floods, earthquakes, and hurricanes); and the threat of worldwide economic debt and nuclear war. (More than ten countries have nuclear weapons: Russia, U.S., France, China, the U.K., Pakistan, India, Israel, North Korea, and Iran.) What are God's promises in times of trouble and distress?

Persevere and stay the course regardless of any opposition or hardship and continue doing what God has called you to do.

Always thank God for His blessings and for creating you in the image of God—and remember the times when God answered your prayers—when He rescued you in times of distress and suffering.

Rely on God's promises and resources:

- Grace of God (2 Timothy 1:2, 9; 2:1).

- **Promises of God** (John 3:16; Matthew 6:33, 7:7; Philippians 4:6-7, 4:13; Psalm 23, 27:1, 37:4, 103:12, 119:105; Romans 6:23, 8:28, 8:38-39, 10:13; 1 John 1:9; Ephesians 2:8-9; Proverbs 3:5-6; John 6:44, 10:27-28, 11:25-26, 14:1-3, 14:6, 15:7; Hebrews 8:12; Genesis 12:3; 1 Thessalonians 4:16-17; Revelation 3:20). God's promises are given to support and maintain our faith through the trials of life and in the "last days" (end times).

- Gift of God—your God-given ability to serve Him (2 Timothy 1:6-7).

- Power of God (instead of your own strength) (2 Timothy 1:8; Philippians 2:13; Ephesians 6:10).

- Indwelling of the Holy Spirit (2 Timothy 1:14).

- Word of God, which provides perspective and understanding (2 Timothy 2:7-9, 3:12-17, 4:1-2).

- What He is preparing for you in heaven (John 14:1-4, 13:36-37; Romans 8:34).

You are not alone in your suffering. You have:

- Presence of Christ (Matthew 28:20).

- Prayers of others (2 Timothy 1:3).

- Others who are facing hardships for the sake of Christ (2 Timothy 1:8; Hebrews 13:3; Colossians 1:24).

- Seek other Christians (in church or prayer groups) whose prayers and encouragement can strengthen you (2 Timothy 1:2, 4-5, 4:9-13, 19-21).

No matter the pain, suffering, and heartache, you can face the future with hope and resolve.

• All wrongs in time will be made right (2 Timothy 3:8-9, 4:14).

• The Lord will deliver you from evil—in His time and way (2 Timothy 4:17-18; Psalm 27).

• All suffering, perseverance, and faithfulness will be rewarded when believers stand before the Lord (2 Timothy 1:12, 18, 2:12, 4:8; Philippians 1:6, 10, 2:16; James 1:12).

• You will give an account of yourself (2 Timothy 1:12, 14; 1 Timothy 6:20).

In suffering, remember the suffering of Jesus Christ (review chapter 8, God's Provision for Sin). Because of sin, no one has suffered more than Jesus, the Son of God.

> *³"He was despised and rejected by mankind, a man of suffering, and familiar with pain. Like one from whom people hide their faces he was despised, and we held him in low esteem.*
>
> *⁴Surely he took up our pain and bore our suffering, yet we considered him punished by God, stricken by him, and afflicted.*
>
> *⁵But he was pierced for our transgressions, he was crushed for our iniquities; the punishment that brought us peace was on him, and by his wounds we are healed.*
>
> *⁶We all, like sheep, have gone astray, each of us has turned to our own way; and the LORD has laid on him the iniquity of us all"* (Isaiah 53:3-6, NIV).
>
> *²³"This man was handed over to you by God's deliberate plan and foreknowledge; and you, with the help of wicked men put him to death by nailing him to the cross. ²⁴But God raised him from the dead, freeing him from the agony of death, because it was impossible for death to keep its hold on him"* (Acts 2:23-24, NIV).
>
> *¹⁸"For you know that it was not with perishable things such as silver or gold that you were redeemed from the empty way of life handed down to you from your ancestors, ¹⁹but with the precious blood of Christ, a lamb without blemish or defect. ²⁰He was chosen before the creation of the world, but was revealed in these last times for your sake. ²¹Through him you believe in God, who raised him from the dead and glorified him, and so your faith and hope are in God"* (1 Peter 1:18-21, NIV).

Suffering, as Jesus Christ suffered during His life on earth, is a process of overcoming a defiant world and submitting to God the Father so we may be glorified together in the afterlife (heaven).

> *"For our light and momentary troubles are achieving for us an eternal glory that far out-weighs them all"* (2 Corinthians 4:17, NIV).
>
> *"And the God of all grace, who called you to his eternal glory in Christ, after you have suffered a little while, will himself restore you and make you strong, firm and steadfast"* (1 Peter 5:10, NIV).
>
> *"I consider that our present sufferings are not worth comparing with the glory that will be revealed in us"* (Romans 8:18, NIV).
>
> *"Not only so, but we also glory in our sufferings, because we know that suffering produces perseverance; perseverance, character; and character, hope"* (Romans 5:3-4, NIV).

In this life suffering is inevitable but don't forget our Lord Jesus Christ. He loves you; He created you; and He will help you. Our finite minds cannot know the purpose for everything, including all evils in the world. We are by nature limited in our knowledge. *"The secret things belong to the Lord our God"* (Deuteronomy 29:29, NIV). The question of evil, pain, and suffering will "ultimately make good sense, in the fullness of time." (Johnson, p. 10)

Appendix C
Is There an Eternal Hell?

> This portion of the book is by far the most difficult to write because this reality is so deeply alarming and horrifying to contemplate—and yet I know that it's true. Although Jesus talked the most about the reality of hell, the primary message of the Bible is not hell but the salvation and eternal life through Jesus Christ.

This subject is hardest to contemplate because sadly, so many people remain unconvinced, apathetic, and unconcerned, and they set aside no time for thoughtful study and prayer—they cling only to their pride and material possessions. But there is nothing more important in this life than the acceptance of the free gift of salvation.

The Bible declares that *"God is love"* (1 John 4:16), and love cannot act forcefully, only gently and persuasively. A God of love cannot make people love Him—to love goodness, holiness, and righteousness. Given "free will" (the freedom to choose for or against God) those who choose against God "must be allowed to be separated. Hell is eternal separation from God." (Geisler, p. 100)

Hell is a place of eternal suffering. John spoke of hell in Revelation 20:11-15; Paul spoke of eternal separation in 2 Thessalonians 1:7-9 and Hebrews 9:27. Hell is outer darkness; a bottomless pit; separation from God (Matthew 8:12, 22:13, 25:41; Mark 9:43-48; Luke 16; Jude 1:13; Revelation 20:1, 3). It is going in the opposite direction of God. People are not forced into separation against their will but rather, it is self-inflicted by one's free will choice of turning away from God.

Jesus acknowledged the existence of hell and warned we should fear both God and hell, *"Do not be afraid of those who kill the body but cannot kill the soul. Rather, be afraid of the One who can destroy both soul and body in hell"* (Matthew 10:28, NIV). He added of those who reject Him, *"As the weeds are pulled up and burned in the fire, so it will be at the end of the age"* (Matthew 13:40, NIV). (Also see Mark 9:43-48.)

The best reason for believing in hell is that Jesus said it exists. "...We cannot repudiate hell without altogether repudiating Christ...Why do I believe in an eternal Hell? Because Jesus clearly and repeatedly affirmed its existence...you cannot dismiss Hell without dismissing Jesus." (Alcorn, p. 311)

So why do so many people reject the "horrifying reality" of hell? There are several reasons: 1) It opposes their personal preference about God (they simply refuse to believe); 2) they have a poor perception of the extent of evil and depravity on earth, and unbelievably, 3) they tend to be indifferent or apathetic about the subject of God, sin, and punishment. **The reality is, the denial of hell is because of their denial of God and God's gift of salvation.**

> [13]*"This is why I speak to them in parables: Though seeing, they do not see; though hearing, they do not hear or understand"* (Matthew 13:13, NIV).

> [10]*"He said, 'the knowledge of the secrets of the kingdom of God has been given to you, but to others I speak in parables,' so that, 'though seeing, they may not see; though hearing, they may not understand'"* (Luke 8:10, NIV).

Our society considers heaven the "default destination" after we die. When did you last attend a funeral in which a pastor spoke of the departed going to hell? Never, they are all going to heaven. But because *"all have sinned and fall short of the glory of God"* (Romans 3:23, NIV), the reality is that all are destined for hell unless the departed have accepted the gift of pardon through the death of Jesus Christ on the Cross of Calvary.

> "The vast majority of those who believe in Hell do not believe they are going there.... This optimism stands in stark contrast to Christ's words in Matthew 7:13-14: 'Enter through the narrow gate. For wide is the gate and broad is the road that leads to destruction, and many enter through it. But small is the gate and narrow the road that leads to life, and only a few find it.'" Such words should be extremely alarming to every rational human being. (Alcorn, p. 318)

I cannot over emphasize the following: **Do not reject the free gift of pardon offered by Jesus Christ**, the promised Messiah, during your time on earth. He stepped out of Eternity (*"His goings forth are from long ago, From the days of eternity,"* Micah 5:2, NAS) and became a guilt offering for mankind. He became a sacrificial 'Lamb of God' on the Cross—the ultimate and final sin offering for the whole world... and bore our iniquities so we can be cleansed of all our sins. He took the penalty for our sins upon Himself—**but we have to believe it, accept it, and receive it in our hearts by faith.**

> *"For it is by grace you have been saved, through faith—and this not from yourselves, it is the gift of God—not by works, so that no one can boast"* (Ephesians 2:8-9, NIV).

"He who believes in Him is not judged; he who does not believe is judged already, because he has not believed in the name of the only begotten Son of God" (John 3:18, NIV).

"For God so loved the world that he gave his only begotten Son, that whosoever believeth in Him should not perish but have everlasting live" (John 3:16, KJV).

> "Life on Earth is a dot, a brief window of opportunity; life in Heaven (and ultimately on the New Earth) is a line going out from that dot for eternity. If we're smart, we'll live not for the dot but for the line." (Alcorn, 2017, p. 1)

When compared to eternity, life here on earth is *"...a mist that appears for a little while and then vanishes"* (James 4:14, NIV).

> By denying hell, we deny the extent of God's holiness and the extent of evil in our world. We deny the extreme seriousness of sin. "Are you tired of all the evil and corruption in this world? Do you long for a world in which such things don't exist? Then you long for a Heaven without evildoers. And that requires either that God **forces** everyone to repent, come to Christ, and embrace his righteousness [a God of love **cannot force people to love Him—to love goodness and holiness**; 'force' and 'love' are a contradiction in terms], or that God provides an alternative residence for those who do not. Hell is that place." [Bold added] (Alcorn, p. 316)

Questions concerning hell:

- If God is all loving, then why punish people at all—some people are born into terrible (dysfunctional) circumstances (e.g., abusive, immoral, or criminal parents, pagan culture, false religion, etc.), so why not just reform people?

    Answer: God does try to reform people; the time of reformation is called life—Planet Earth - God's Testing Ground. Some people are unwilling to reform—hell is for the unreformable and unrepentant. God is omnipresent, omnipotent, and omniscient, and **He knows a person's heart** and if they can be reformed if given the opportunity.

- Why did God create people He knew would go to hell? Or is it fair to send people to hell when they can't help being born into sin?

    Answer: During this life God gives people opportunity to turn to Him. Although some are born into very difficult circumstances, there is always a clear path and they make choices for or against God, so they are *"without excuse"* (Romans 1:19-20, 2:12-15).

    "In the past God overlooked such ignorance [God had not judged them for worshipping false gods in their ignorance]*, but now he commands all people everywhere to repent"* (Acts 17:30, NIV). All people are responsible for their decision to accept or reject God's free gift of pardon. God will get the message to them but *"without faith it is impossible to please God, because* **anyone who comes to him must believe that he exists and that he rewards those who earnestly seek him***"* (Hebrews 11:6; Acts 17:26-28, NIV). [Bold added]

- Why have a hell at all—why not just annihilate those who choose to reject God? Why doesn't God eliminate (annihilate) those He knew would embrace evil?

    Answer: God cannot demand that you either love me or I'll annihilate (kill) you—this is of course illogical.

- Even if punishment is justified, why punish people forever—isn't this an extreme overkill? A forever hell seems excessive or extreme. Why not have a purgatory followed by another testing period?

    Answer: Heaven demands a hell. Without separation of the 'wheat and the tares' (Matthew 13:30), there would be no heaven. Evil, if not contained, will continue to infect and corrupt. The 'sheep and the goats' must be separated (Matthew 25:32-34); otherwise, there is no final victory over evil (cf 1 Corinthians 15:24-28; Revelation 20-22).

- The Cross is at the center of Christianity (1 Corinthians 1:17-18, 15:3)—and without the Cross there is no salvation (Romans 4:25; Hebrews 10:10-14; Acts 4:12; John 10:1, 9-10). Then why the Cross and the terrible suffering of Christ?

    Answer: The Cross of Christ demands a hell. God decided before laying the foundation of the world **He would rather endure the horrible and agonizing suffering on the Cross at the hands of sinful men on our behalf rather than forsake the creation of mankind.**

The purpose of Jesus dying on the Cross for our sins (as a sacrificial lamb, bearing the sins of humanity and offering the free gift of pardon by simply turning to God) was to preserve freedom and love, rid the universe of evil forever, and start a divine family in His image in Heaven. The Cross assures the defeat of Satan and evil. *"The reason the Son of God appeared was to destroy the devil's work"* (1 John 3:8, NIV).

> Jesus Christ is referred to as *"the firstborn among many brethren"* (Romans 8:29, NAS; see also Romans 8:14-17; Revelation 1:5-6; Colossians 1:15-18). He came as a human being to lead the way for others to be glorified and inherit all things. Christians are actually referred to as *"...**heirs of God and joint heirs with Christ, if indeed we share in His sufferings in order that we may also share in His glory**"* (Romans 8:17, NIV). [Bold added]

Again, without a hell there could be no Heaven. In God's eyes mankind must be extremely valuable, and by paying such a high price for us (humankind in our present depraved state) emphasizes the extent of His love. **The price has been paid, but we can't benefit from His forgiveness unless we choose to receive the free gift of pardon and repent of our sins.**

God guarantees, in advance, complete and ultimate victory over evil (Revelation 21-22) but unless there is a hell, there is no final victory. For some people, no matter what, they will say no to God. A God of love cannot force people to love Him—to love goodness. Without a hell, it would make the Cross and the gift of pardon irrelevant. Apart from Christ we would all spend eternity in hell.

What About Truly Good and Gentle People Who Have Never Repented and Accepted the Gift of Pardon?

> For those who are concerned about loved ones, those who were dear, loving, gentle, and vulnerable in this life but may have never made a commitment to Jesus Christ, please be assured that God is loving, just, merciful, and holy (Isaiah 6:1-3; Psalm 99:5; Habakkuk 1:13; Psalm 5:5-6; Isaiah 57:15; and Leviticus 20:26; Matthew 5:7; Samuel 22:26; 1 Peter 3-4; John 3:16, 5:24, 14:6; Romans 10:9, 13), and <u>He will always make a just, merciful, and righteous decision about every individual</u>. The Lord is omniscient, omnipotent, and omnipresent (Romans 8:29; Ephesians 1:4-5; 1 Corinthians 2:7)—even before the beginning of time, God foreknew the choice you would make, although you still have freedom of choice today. The Lord knows each one of us and the **inclinations of our heart**, and <u>He will always make the right and just decision</u> (see 2 Peter 3:9; 1 Timothy 2:4).

While belief in and acceptance of Jesus Christ is indeed essential for salvation (John 14:6; Acts 4:12), there remains the question: What happens to those genuinely good and gentle people who may have slipped through the cracks—people who, for one reason or another, never made a genuine commitment because of life's circumstances—they were either deceived (Revelation 12:9) or they lacked sufficient understanding of Jesus Christ, the Cross, repentance, and the free gift of pardon, or perhaps a thousand other reasons?

Surely, in this life there are so many situations that could lead someone away from Jesus Christ: unloving or abusive parents; raised and indoctrinated in a false religion; or dying too early without the chance to truly understand Christianity; blaming God for the loss of a loved one through terrible pain and suffering; and the list goes on. And what about those who, in recent years or in centuries past, lived and died without ever hearing the name of Jesus Christ? Are such people eternally lost?

The Bible gives the answers to these questions—answers that reconcile all the Scriptures about life and death, judgment and mercy, forgiveness and salvation. It reveals that the "first resurrection" of Christ's followers at His return is not the end of the story.

The Great White Throne Judgment, described in Revelation 20:11-13, is the judgment of human beings following the 1000 year Millennial Period (see pgs. 185 and 199-200, in the book, *World in Denial – Defiant Nature of Mankind*) who are not found in the Book of Life—people who have either defiantly rejected the gift of pardon while on earth **or those who have died <u>without</u> a spirit of defiance and <u>not fully understanding</u> the plan of salvation through Jesus Christ.**

Those who have **<u>defiantly rejected</u>** the gift of pardon *are "without excuse"* (Romans 1:19-20; cf. 2:12-15)—they will be evaluated and judged and assigned a place in hell. Others who died without a spirit of defiance and not fully understanding the great plan and their need for repentance will fully learn His truth.

This judgment is an opportunity for many to fully understand and undergo evaluation as opposed to an act of condemnation and sentencing. Those of the second group will stand before God and have the full truth of the Scriptures opened to their understanding (Revelation 20:4-6, 11-12). I believe that God will extend the atonement of Christ to cover them.

This biblical resurrection to judgment (a time for sorting out and deciding; not automatic condemnation) is a time when God's loving mercy will finally be evident to all who are willing to face up to and repent of their former sins. For a majority of mankind, this may be their first real opportunity to fully comprehend God's truth and then make a "free will" decision.

> "For those who die young or may otherwise lack the mental capacity to respond to Christ [or due to other life circumstances of which there may be thousands] many Christians throughout the ages have believed God may extend the atonement of Christ to cover them as an act of grace. I agree." The Lord is omniscient, omnipotent, and omnipresent—even before the beginning of time, God foreknew the choice you would make, although you still have freedom of choice. (Alcorn, p. 319)

Most will sincerely acknowledge their errors, ask for forgiveness and repent, and many will be glorified and receive eternal life. Others will 'harden their hearts' (Ephesians 4:18) like those of the first group who fully rejected the gift of pardon while on earth, and they will be sentenced to hell based on their sinful deeds while on earth.

All sinners need to do is to repent (Acts 17:30). All are held responsible for their decision to accept or reject God's offer of salvation. *"Without faith it is impossible to please God, because **anyone who comes to him must believe that he exists and that he rewards those who earnestly seek him**"* (Hebrews 11:6, NIV). [Bold added]

This world is in a state of immorality and depravity and all are sinful to one degree or another, *"For all have sinned and fall short of the glory of God"* (Romans 3:23, NIV). The times in which we live are getting worse, as in the days of Noah. The message of the Bible and creation cry out, "There is a God" and you must act while you can. Inexplicably, many in today's world simply turn away from God and will not accept the gift of salvation.

> God in his wisdom and goodness would not allow anyone to go to hell who He knew would go to heaven if He gave more opportunity (2 Peter 3:9); He *"wants all men to be saved..."* (1 Timothy 2:4, NIV).

https://www.ucg.org/bible-study-tools/bible-questions-and-answers/what-happens-to-all-of-mankind-who-lived-and-died

This short response gives only a brief overview of a great biblical truth revealing God's mercy regarding untold billions who have died without understanding forgiveness through Jesus Christ. Are they lost forever? Or does God have a way for them to possibly still be saved?

Appendix D
Evidence for the Existence of God

Scientific Evidence for Divine Creation

For more information on this important subject, see the book by Roger Gallop,
evolution - The Greatest Deception in Modern History (Scientific Evidence for Divine Creation).

One would logically theorize that in an infinite universe, with no valid (verifiable) explanation as to the cause, a supernatural cause would certainly be a real or certain possibility—the only logical possibility. Nevertheless, secular scientists today are totally dedicated to a naturalistic explanation of origin although they have to "explain how nothing became everything" and thereby "invoke their own supernatural 'first act.'" (Bates) For whatever reason, if a person's mind is closed to Scripture, no amount of evidence (scientific and theological) will change his or her mind.

> Evolution is a belief system that many, if not most, scientists assume as fact and routinely use to interpret their observations. Instead of gathering scientific data and forming a conclusion (i.e., using the scientific method: observation, prediction, data collection, experimentation [to test the hypothesis under controlled conditions], and conclusions), evolutionists form their conclusions and then search for evidence to support it.

Dr. Henry M. Morris, Ph.D., once stated, "The fact is that evolutionists believe in evolution because they want to. It is their desire at all costs to explain the origin of everything without a Creator. Evolutionism is thus intrinsically an atheistic religion.... Whether atheism or humanism (or even pantheism), the purpose is to eliminate a personal God from any active role in the origin of the universe and all its components, including man." (Morris, H.M.)

What many people today never hear and realize is the fact that scientific creation is based on scientific evidence—and such evidence is **overwhelming.** So why do secular scientists continue to adhere to a false evolutionary doctrine? The book by Roger Gallop, *evolution – The Greatest Deception in Modern History,* provides some of the reasons (see epilogue, pp. 216-218) and summarizes much of the evidence for scientific creation, including research by esteemed scientists in almost all fields of science listed below.

- Evolution is contrary to the First and Second Laws of Thermodynamics (see chapter 2), the Law of Biogenesis (see chapter 3), and the Law of Causality whereas creation is consistent with such laws. These laws have always proved valid whenever tested. Many scientists believe the 2nd Law is enough to disprove evolutionary theory and is one of the important reasons why many esteemed scientists have abandoned evolutionary doctrine in favor of creationism.

- Students in public schools (middle-high schools, colleges, and universities) are taught as scientific fact that "survival of the fittest" caused evolution of life on Earth—but this is a complete falsehood. Natural selection (or survival of the fittest, adaptation, or speciation) is, in fact, a 'thinning out process' that leads to loss of genetic information.

- Evolution has no known biological processes or mechanisms to form higher levels of organization and complexity—gene mutations are overwhelmingly degenerative and none are "uphill" (i.e., unequivocally beneficial) in the sense of adding new genetic information to the gene pool.

- The probability of getting an average-size protein of left-handed amino acids (found only in living cells) by random, natural processes is **zero**. And the probability of getting a living cell, synonymous to the most sophisticated supercomputer yet microscopic in size, is likewise **zero**, and consciousness (awareness, perception) would only be expected from a Divine creator.

- Geologic landforms and sedimentary features throughout the world are completely consistent with a worldwide flood as described in the Book of Genesis. For many esteemed geologists who have researched geologic landforms and catastrophic processes, evidence of a global flood is **indisputable**.

- A worldwide flood as described in Genesis 6-8 is within the boundaries of known geophysics—see phase diagram in chapter 4 of the book, *evolution – The Greatest Deception in Modern History* and **Pangaea Flood Video at www.CreationScienceToday.com**.

- Enormous limestone formations, huge coal and oil formations, and immense underground salt layers are indicative of a worldwide flood—*not slow and gradual processes over billions of years*. Such features are satisfactorily explained by a global flood and known geophysical and geochemical processes.

- There is no credible technique for establishing the age of sedimentary rock—fossil dating used to establish the age of sedimentary rock suffers from circular reasoning and guesswork, all based on the assumption of evolution.

- The standard geologic and fossil column, as depicted in most science textbooks with transitional creatures evolving toward more complex forms, is utterly fictitious and misleading and does not represent the real world. In reality, it perfectly represents the aftermath of a worldwide flood.

- There are no transitional fossils or living forms—there is not one single example of evolution! Evolutionists look for "the" missing link—ironically, they are in desperate search for just one! But there should be billions of examples of transitional forms with transitional structures if evolution were true, but there are none. The bottom line, evolution has never been observed within fossils or living populations.

- Irreducible complexity (IC) is another reason why evolution is impossible. A practical household analogy is the common mousetrap—its individual parts have no transitional value or function yet the trap could not function if any of the parts were missing. A biological example is the human eye comprising the iris, pupil, cornea, sclera, lens, macula, retina, optic disk, and optic nerve. The individual parts have no value yet the eye could not function if any of the parts were missing. Amniotic eggs and the flagellum of bacteria are other examples of IC. These and other biologic systems of the body could not have evolved piece by piece (according to Darwinian gradualism) because the entire system must be present at the start for the system to work.

- Contrary to popular belief, evidence indicates that early man was intelligent and highly skilled with an advanced social structure. There is also evidence suggesting their belief in the existence of an afterlife.

- Soft tissue with traces of red blood cells has been found in dinosaur fossils supposedly 70 to 250 million years old, but soft tissue and red blood cells have relative short life spans.

- Carbon-14 has been found in coal and diamonds and in deep geological strata, all supposedly hundreds of millions of years old. Researchers have been unable to find carbon (stable forms: carbon-12 and -13) without carbon-14 (unstable form). (C-14 has a relatively short life span.)

- Radioisotope dating suffers from broken, unprovable assumptions. The technique is "fatally flawed"—yet scientists contend as fact what they cannot prove primarily because of their desire to explain the origin of the universe without a Creator.

- Abundant daughter isotopes are indicative of accelerated nuclear decay associated with creation (expansion, stretching out, or acceleration of the universe from an extremely hot, dense phase when matter and energy were concentrated) and a worldwide flood with massive restructuring of the earth's lithosphere—*not slow and gradual processes over billions of years*.

- Powerful evidences of accelerated nuclear decay in igneous rocks found worldwide are helium in zircon crystals, radiohalos and fission tracks, and rapid magnetic field reversals and decay.

- Gravitational time dilation offers a credible explanation for a young earth—that is, it explains how light from the extremities of the universe has the potential of reaching the earth in a relatively short period of time (from earth's perspective).

- Over a hundred geochronometers (techniques to date the earth and universe) indicate a young earth and universe (e.g., helium in zircon crystals, rapid magnetic field reversals and decay, carbon-14 found in coal and diamonds, and lack of continental erosion, lack of ocean sediments, and lack of salt in the sea).

Each one of these evidences is enough to convince most rational people that evolution is a false doctrine and the earth is, in fact, young!

The Bible's Prophetic Accuracy

For more information on this subject, see the book, *World in Denial – Defiant Nature of Mankind (Prophetic Evidence for a Divine Creator)*.

Prophecy is "history written in advance"—and could only be given by the omnipresent, omnipotent, and omniscient God of the Holy Bible. The apostle Peter states in 2 Peter 1:21 (NIV), *"For prophecy never had its origin in the human will, but prophets, though human, spoke from God as they were carried along by the Holy Spirit."*

People today can look no farther than Biblical prophecy to see God working in our world—**yet most people are completely**

Biblical prophecy plays two roles. It foretells future events, and it explains positive or negative results. Prophecy announces events that bring joy and pleasure or fear and foreboding. When prophecy is ignored, it is usually because people don't like what they hear. Biblical prophecy is always accurate and precise.

In Matthew 24 Jesus spoke of wars, famines, earthquakes, persecutions, apostasy, and betrayals in the last days, and finally of His own return, but most incredibly even in light of current worldwide events including the rebirth of the State of Israel and its possession of the City of Jerusalem (see chapters 6 - 10 of the above forementioned book), such prophecy is widely rejected today. This and other end time prophecies are as dependable as Noah's warning of the Flood. Read and consider 2 Peter 3:3-10: a modern day warning!

unaware of such miraculous events. Jesus described this inability to understand as *"though seeing, they may not see; though hearing, they may not understand"* (Luke 8:10-12, NIV; Matthew 13:14). Fulfilled prophecies that we can actually see today provide some of the strongest reasons to believe the Truth of the Holy Bible and are evidence proving the Bible's credibility as a product of supernatural Divine Creation.

Prophecy illustrates the power of God through the fulfillment of impossible predictions—specific human events predicted thousands of years in advance—events that we can see and understand today. Wilbur Smith, worldwide bestselling author, concludes that: (Smith)

> "...whatever one may think of the authority of and the message presented in the book we call the Bible, there is worldwide agreement that in more ways than one it is the most remarkable volume [book] that has ever been produced in these some five thousand years of writing on the part of the human race."

> "It is the only volume ever produced by man, or a group of men in which is to be found a large body of prophecies relating to individual nations, to Israel, to all the peoples of the earth, to certain cities, and to the coming One who was to be the Messiah. The ancient world had many different devices for determining the future, known as divination, but not in the entire gamut of Greek and Latin literature, even though they use the words prophet and prophecy, can we find any real specific prophecy of a great historic event to come in the distant future, nor any prophecy of a Savior to arise in the human race..."

> "Mohammedanism cannot point to any prophecies of the coming of Mohammed uttered hundreds of years before his birth. Neither can the founders of any cult in this country rightly identify any ancient text specifically foretelling their appearance."

> The Bible is God-breathed (2 Timothy 3:16; 2 Peter 1:21; Genesis 2:7; Exodus 24:3-4, 7; Jeremiah 36:1-4; 1 Corinthians 14:37; Revelation 1:1, 2, 10-11, 19; and Ephesians 3:3-5). All Scripture is inspired by God and was given through Old Testament prophets and New Testament apostles to instruct men how to live righteously before God.
>
> About 33 percent of the Bible focuses on prophecy, and the majority of these prophecies focus on the amazing end time prophecies happening in today's world: the rebirth of the State of Israel, the nations of the world, signs of the end times, the rapture of the church, the seven year tribulation period, and the Second Coming of our Lord Jesus Christ.
>
> Prophecy concerning the history of Israel and current end time events is found in the Major Prophets (Isaiah, Jeremiah, Ezekiel, and Daniel) and Minor Prophets (Hosea, Joel, Amos, Asaph, Obadiah, Jonah, Micah, Nahum, Habakkuk, Zephaniah, Haggai, Zechariah, and Malachi) of the Old Testament. End time prophecy in the New Testament is found in Matthew, Mark, Luke, John, First and Second Thessalonians, First and Second Timothy, First and Second Peter, and Revelation.

Many people "attack predictive prophecy from the viewpoint of post-dating," that is, writing the prophecy after the event rather than before. Josh McDowell, in his book, *Evidence that Demands a Verdict*, shows how these Biblical prophecies are NOT "post-dictions" (that is, written after the event). (McDowell, p. 280) Ancient hand-written scrolls were copied and recopied and then distributed and redistributed throughout the known world of that time. It is logical to understand that no one could possibly have collected all the copies, from Egypt to Babylon to Greece, to make modifications after the event. And enough copies have been found among ancient artifacts during archaeological excavations to confirm they were written long before the events were accurately prophesied.

The most prominent super sign of the end times is the rebirth of the State of Israel on May 14, 1948. After being scattered throughout the world for 1,878 years (AD 70 – 1948) with no territory, homeland or nation of their own, Israel was recognized as a sovereign state in 1948 for the first time since AD 70. After nearly 2,000 years the Jews were **miraculously** restored to their ancient homeland (in just one day) in direct fulfillment of Bible prophecy (Deuteronomy 30:1-5; Isaiah 43:5-7, 66:7-8; Ezekiel 34:13, 36:22-24, 37:1-6, 11-14, 21-23, 39:27-29; Hosea 3:4-5; Jeremiah 31:10, 31:35-36; and Amos 9:14-15).

Continual disobedience, lack of repentance, defiance, worship of pagan idols, and ultimately, rejection of the Messiah, Jesus Christ, led to worldwide exile of the Jewish people beginning AD 70 when the Romans destroyed the Second Temple. The Jewish people were forewarned of **an exile in which they would be scattered from one end of the earth to the other. Moses first prophesied this great dispersion** in Leviticus 26:31-33 and then in Deuteronomy 28:64-68, 30:15. (See chapter 3, Punishment for Disobedience and Moses Predicts the Future, in the book, *World in Denial - Defiant Nature of Mankind.*) The contents of Leviticus and Deuteronomy were given to Moses by God on Mount Sinai.

Ultimately, **Israel's rejection of Jesus of Nazareth as the coming Messiah** foretold in Isaiah 53:2-7 (fulfilled in John 7:5, 48-49; also see John 1:11; Matthew 21:42-43) **was the cause of the Jewish worldwide Diaspora.** As a result, the Jews lost their "Promised Land" for nearly two thousand years, and they lost their status as *"a people holy to the LORD."*

The rebirth of Israel and repossession of the ancient City of Jerusalem following the Six Day War on June 5–10, 1967 (prerequisites to rebuilding the Temple and the Second Coming), are pre-tribulation super signs. Many other end time prophetic events pertaining to Israel and surrounding countries (European Union, Russia, Iran, Arab countries, and China) are currently being fulfilled in today's world, but most people are oblivious to end time Bible prophecy.

A professor once remarked to J. McDowell, "If you are an intelligent man, you will read the one book that has drawn more attention than any other, if you are searching for the truth." (McDowell, 26)
If you are seeking the truth about what is going on in the world today, then read the Bible.

The Bible's Unity

The Bible comprises 39 Old Testament Books and 27 New Testament Books and was written over a span of nearly 1600 years by more than 40 authors from various occupations and social classes including kings, peasants, philosophers, fishermen, herdsmen, physicians, businessmen, poets, statesmen, scholars, military generals, etc. (beginning with Genesis and the Torah written by Moses about 1450 BC and ending with Revelation written by the apostle John about AD 95).

Furthermore, the Bible was written in different places: Moses in the wilderness; Jeremiah in a dungeon; Daniel in a palace (ruins have been discovered; see chapter 3, United Kingdom, in the book, *World in Denial – Defiant Nature of Mankind*); Paul inside a Roman prison; Luke while traveling; John on the Isle of Patmos, a small Greek island in the Aegean Sea; and others during military crusades; in different times (David in times of war and Solomon in times of peace); different moods (times of joy and during times of great sorrow and despair); on different continents (Asia, Africa, and Europe); and in three languages (Hebrew-Old Testament, Aramaic-language of Christ, and Greek-New Testament).

The Bible is consistent in its message and form (composition, symmetry, style, and agreement) from beginning to end: creation and fall of mankind (Genesis), disobedience and moral depravity of mankind (throughout the Old and New Testaments), and God reaching out to mankind offering redemption or a bridge to salvation (New Testament). The theme throughout the Bible is 'God's plan of redemption' for sinful and immoral humanity.

> The Bible's major categories and books: Creation (Genesis); Law (Exodus through Deuteronomy); History (Joshua through Esther); Poetry (Job through Song of Solomon); Major Prophets (Moses, Isaiah, Jeremiah, Ezekiel, and Daniel); Minor Prophets (Hosea, Joel, Amos, Asaph, Obadiah, Jonah, Micah, Nahum, Habakkuk, Zephaniah, Haggai, Zechariah, and Malachi); Life of Christ (Matthew, Mark, Luke, and John); History of the church (Acts); Epistles and Letters (Romans through Jude); and Prophecy (Revelation).

The first and last Books of the Bible—Genesis and Revelation, written by Moses and John, respectively—fit together perfectly in describing "paradise lost" and "paradise regained"—in Genesis 1-3 and Revelation 21-22. From the first book of Genesis to the last book of Revelation, the Bible is perfectly unified, impeccably written, and the most widely distributed book of all time. Mere human genius could never have accomplished such an extraordinary feat. (Ham, et al, p. 17) Such unity is humanly impossible—man with his immoral nature, arrogance, and self-absorption could not have written this book.

According to Scripture, the Bible is God-breathed (2 Timothy 3:16; 2 Peter 1:21; Genesis 2:7; Exodus 24:3, 4, 7; Jeremiah 36:1-4; 1 Corinthians 14:37; Revelation 1:1, 2, 10, 11, 19; and Ephesians 3:3-5). Although 2 Timothy 3:16 is the only place in the Bible where the phrase "God-breathed" is used, Scripture is filled with similar meanings. All Scripture is inspired by God and was given through Old Testament prophets and New Testament apostles to instruct men how to live righteously before God.

The late Dr. David L. Cooper, one of the most esteemed Bible scholars in the world, said of the Bible, "Abundant and overwhelming is the proof that the Scriptures are God-breathed. No open-minded truth-seeker can weigh the evidence for the divine origin of the Scriptures and can arrive at the conclusion that the books of the Bible were written by uninspired men." (Cooper, p. 7)

The Bible's Historical Accuracy

If the Bible is divinely inspired, it must be historically accurate—and if the Bible is accurate, then this is strong evidence that the authors were divinely inspired. Over the last several hundred years, enemies of Christianity have attacked the Bible's historical accuracy but, in every case, the Bible has been proved correct through archaeological excavations: stone ruins, relics, monuments, tombs, and artifacts of ancient civilizations. Peoples and events, known only previously in Scripture, have been verified through such excavations and, in every instance, the Bible has always been proven right. (Sasser)

The Old and New Testaments make abundant references to nations, kings, battles, cities, rivers and mountains, buildings, customs, politics, dates, etc. Because historical accounts described in the Bible are so specific, many details are subject to archaeological examination and verification. Critics in the 19th century made many accusations in an attempt to disprove the reliability of the Bible but the astonishing increase of archaeological facts in the 20th century has overturned all these skeptical claims.

> Archaeology is the study of human activity in the past, primarily through the recovery and analysis of material culture such as relics, monuments, inscriptions, tombs, and artifacts of ancient civilizations.

Archaeological discoveries this past century have confirmed many hundreds of biblical statements. Dr. Henry M. Morris concluded his study of archeological evidence of the Bible by stating, "It must be extremely significant that, in view of the great mass of corroborative evidence regarding the Biblical history of these periods, there exists today not one unquestionable find of archaeology that proves the Bible to be in error at any point." (Morris, H.M.)

Nelson Glueck, renowned Jewish archaeologist, wrote that "It may be stated categorically that no archaeological discovery has ever controverted a biblical reference." He continued by stating "...the almost incredibly accurate historical memory of the Bible, and particularly so when it is fortified by archaeological fact." (Glueck, p. 31) Josh McDowell, in his book, *Evidence that Demands a Verdict,* cites example after example of esteemed archaeologists and historians who attest to the accuracy of the Bible.

William F. Albright, one of our great archaeologists, states that "There can be no doubt that archaeology has confirmed the substantial historicity of Old Testament tradition." Albright adds, "Discovery after discovery has established the accuracy of innumerable details, and has brought increased recognition to the value of the Bible as a source of history." (Albright; cited McDowell, p. 68)

The late Millar Burrows, an American biblical scholar, a leading authority on the Dead Sea scrolls, and professor emeritus at the Yale Divinity School, explained the cause of excessive unbelief by stating, "The excessive skepticism of many liberal theologians stems not from a careful evaluation of the available data, but from *an enormous predisposition against the supernatural.*" [Italics added] (Burrows, p. 291) (Then I must ask the question, why are there theologians?)

The Bible's Preservation

The Bible was preserved through a process called canonization. Our English word canonization comes from the Greek word kanon, which means 'a straight edge or ruler.' In other words it is a rigorous review process using precise rules and standards.

The books of the Bible have been canonized and have been determined to be Holy Scripture, or the divinely inspired Word of God. Canonization could not have been done without using such standards. "Determining the standards was a process conducted first by Jewish rabbis and scholars and then later by early Christians. Ultimately, it was God who decided which books belonged in the biblical canon." (Got Questions, Canon-Bible)

Old Testament

Because of this extreme care, the quality of Hebrew manuscripts exceeds all other ancient documents. The 1947 discovery of the Dead Sea Scrolls provided a significant check or verification of the accuracy because these ancient scrolls predate (exist before) the earliest Masoretic Old Testament manuscripts by about 1,000 years. Regardless of this time span, the number of alternative interpretations between the Dead Sea Scrolls and the Masoretic Text is very small, and most are slight changes in spelling and style. As Sir Frederic Kenyon said, "the Christian can take the whole Bible in his hand and say without fear or hesitation that he holds in it the true Word of God, handed down without essential loss from generation to generation throughout the centuries." (Kenyon, p. 25)

As explained by Dr. Kenneth Boa, "Because of the great reverence the Jewish scribes held toward the Scriptures, they exercised extreme care in making new copies of the Hebrew Bible. The entire scribal process was specified in meticulous detail to minimize the possibility of even the slightest error. The number of letters, words, and lines were counted, and the middle letters of the Pentateuch and the Old Testament were determined. If a single mistake was discovered, the entire manuscript would be destroyed." (Boa, K.)

The late Robert D. Wilson, an American linguist and Presbyterian scholar who devoted his life to studying and proving the reliability of the Hebrew Bible (Old Testament), states: "In 144 cases of transliteration from Egyptian, Assyrian, Babylonian, and Moabite into Hebrew and in 40 cases of the opposite, or 184 cases in all, the evidence shows that for 2,300 to 3,900 years the text of the proper names in the Hebrew Bible has been transmitted with the most minute accuracy. That the original scribes should have written them with such close conformity to correct philological [lingual, dialectal] principles is a wonderful proof of their thorough care and scholarship; further that the Hebrew text should have been transmitted by copyists through so many centuries is a phenomenon unequalled in the history of literature." (Wilson; as cited in McDowell, p. 58)

For more information, see chapter 1 of the book, *World in Denial - Defiant Nature of Mankind (Prophetic Evidence for a Divine Creator)*.

Dead Sea Scroll, Book of Isaiah, found in the Ancient Caves at Qumran near the Dead Sea. *Photo by Roger Gallop, March 11, 2016*

New Testament

The quantity of New Testament manuscripts is unsurpassed in ancient literature. There are about 8,000 Latin manuscripts, over 5,000 Greek manuscripts, and at least 1,000 in other languages. "In regard to the New Testament there are about thirteen thousand manuscripts, complete and incomplete, in Greek and other languages that have survived from antiquity. No other works from classical antiquity has such attestation." (Ramm, p. 230) In comparison, the usual number of existing manuscripts for works of Greek and Latin authors, such as Plato, Aristotle or Caesar, ranges from 1 to 20.

Scripture has been translated into hundreds of languages (both ancient and modern)—and comparisons can be made to determine the possibility of errors or changes. Such extensive comparisons of these ancient manuscripts have found very little variance. Of this little variance, "only a small number of these differences affect the sense of the passages, and only a fraction of these have any real consequences." (Boa, K.) Many of the earliest surviving manuscripts (such as Syriac and Coptic versions) show that God's Word has been precisely preserved in many languages.

According to Josh McDowell, "After trying to shatter the historicity and validity of the Scripture, I came to the conclusion that they [ancient manuscripts] are historically trustworthy. If one disregards the Bible as being unreliable, then he must disregard almost all literature of antiquity." (McDowell, p. 76)

The Bible's Uniqueness

Why has the Bible become the most widely distributed and most influential book of all time? And what are the chances that such a small nation of people (Israel) would write a book that would have the greatest influence worldwide? Certainly, the odds for such a book would favor a more ancient society such as Egypt, Mesopotamia (cradle of civilization), or any one of the other great empires. (Konig, p. 1-3)

But instead, the world's most prominent and influential book comes from the Jewish people of tiny Israel—who from the time of Moses and all the major and minor prophets until the time of Jesus and His apostles (a span of more than 1,600 years) was inspired by God (God-breathed; 2 Timothy 3:16; 2 Peter 1:21; Genesis 2:7; Exodus 24:3, 4, 7; Jeremiah 36:1-4; 1 Corinthians 14:37; Revelation 1:1, 2, 10, 11, 19; and Ephesians 3:3-5) to record the words of the Bible through the prophets, disciples, and apostles. And these words included assurances and prophecies that information about God would reach the ends of the earth. (Konig, p. 1-3)

In addition, Jesus stated in Matthew 24:14 and Mark 13:10 that His words would spread around the world. And in Psalm 48:10 and Psalm 22:27 are references to God being known and praised throughout the world and in Isaiah 45:22 is the offer of salvation to all people. The Bible became the first religious book to be distributed worldwide and is the predominant religious book in Europe, and North and South America; also, it has an influential presence throughout Africa, Asia including Hong Kong, the Philippines, Russia, and South Korea. (Konig, p. 1-3)

The Moral Law

Some people (who do not understand "free will"; see chapters 7 and 8) claim there is no God because there is so much evil in the world – but by what moral code do we call something evil? We can't call something evil unless we have a sense of what is good, holy, and righteous. We don't know something is unjust unless we know what is just – and this leads us to the Moral Law.

When we discuss the laws of nature we usually refer to the laws of chemistry, physics, and biology. Such laws include thermodynamics, gravitation, motion, fluid dynamics, buoyancy, elasticity, partial pressure, biogenesis, and heredity. But there is another law that is just as valid—a Moral Law that was examined by C. S. Lewis in his book, *Mere Christianity*—a universal law of decent behavior or morality—a law of "right and wrong" behavior. Unlike other natural laws, the Moral Law is a law that human beings are free to disobey. (Lewis, C.S.) (See Nature of Mankind, Prologue of the book, *World in Denial - Defiant Nature of Mankind*.)

Since the rebellion of Adam, humanity has had an inherited or inborn tendency to sin and rebel—to oppose the Creator's sovereignty over their lives. In the days of Noah (4004 BC – 2385 BC), mankind was rebellious and exceedingly wicked—and with this came eventual consequences—the Flood that destroyed all of humanity. Rebellion and wickedness have been continually present throughout the history of mankind. (See chapters 5 and 6.)

In opposition to this tendency, the Moral Law motivates humans to make personal sacrifices that may lead to suffering, injury, and even death without the possibility of personal benefit. Such behavior is in direct conflict with apes (nonhuman primates) and other animals. According to Lewis, man has two impulses: the first is to provide help and the second is to avoid danger, but the overriding drive is to help—not to run away. (p. 9-10) Although we are free to disobey (free will) this inner voice of conscience, the motivation to do the right thing is real. The Moral Law will ask me to save a drowning man with personal sacrifice, even if he is an enemy or stranger. (p. 10)

The reality is, not one person keeps the Moral Law all the time and many of us never keep the law at all—and in the act of not keeping the law, most humans *try to shift the blame or alleviate their wrong behavior with all types of excuses.* Quarrelling between two individuals, for example, is "appealing to some kind of standard of behavior which he expects the other man to know about." (p. 3) Lewis sums it up: "human beings, all over the world, have this curious idea that they ought to behave in a certain way...[but] they do not in fact behave in that way." (p. 8) The question is, what lies behind this law? (p. 13)

As Lewis explains, "If there was a controlling power outside the universe, it could not show itself to us as one of the facts inside the universe—no more than the architect of a house could actually be a wall or staircase or fireplace in that house. The only way in which we could expect it to show itself would be inside ourselves as an influence or a command trying to get us to behave in a certain way. And that is just what we do find inside ourselves. Surely this ought to arouse our suspicions?" (p. 24) [Italics added]

God wants man to behave in a certain way, urging man to do what is right and just, and if he does not, he is made to feel uncomfortable. (p. 23) One must conclude that this must be a holy and righteous God who despises evil. This is certainly proclaimed throughout the Bible. If God is outside the universe—outside the natural world—the tools of science cannot find God. Ultimately, the decision to acknowledge and accept God is based on personal choice and faith (Matthew 17:20; Romans 1:17, 3:22, 3:28; and 2 Corinthians 5:7, NIV, *"We live by faith, not by sight"*).

Attempts to Destroy the Bible

Over the many centuries the Bible has withstood fierce attacks like no other book in history. Many have tried to burn it or ban it, and "outlaw it from the days of Roman emperors to present-day Communist dominated countries." (Ramm, p. 232) Despite vicious attacks and efforts to destroy the Bible, it remains the greatest book throughout all time.

Greek ruler Antiochus Epiphanes, who ruled the Seleucid Empire (Syrian region of Judah) from c. 175 BC to 164 BC, tried to eradicate Judaism (the religion, culture, and way of life of the Jewish people) by destroying all copies of the Torah, the first five books of the Bible. He also defiled the Temple in Jerusalem; he ordered the killing of tens of thousands of Jewish men, women, and children; and he ordered the Jews to destroy their Hebrew Scripture and worship Zeus as their supreme god.

Another example is the Roman emperor Diocletian who issued an edict in AD 303 to kill all Christians and destroy their Bibles: "... an imperial letter was everywhere promulgated, ordering the razing of the churches to the ground and the destruction by fire of the Scriptures, proclaiming that those who held high positions would lose all civil rights, while those in households, if they persisted in their profession of Christianity, would be deprived of their liberty." (McDowell, p. 23)

In his book, *All About the Bible*, author Sidney Collett says "Voltaire, the noted French infidel who died in 1778, said that in one hundred years from his time Christianity would be swept from existence and passed into history. But what has happened? Voltaire has passed into history; while the circulation of the Bible continues to increase in almost all parts of the world, carrying blessing wherever it goes." (Collet, p. 63)

Jesus Christ made a remarkable prophecy about the preservation of His Word: *"Heaven and earth will pass away, but My words will never pass away"* (Mark 13:31, NIV; also Matthew 24:35). God's Word is indestructible: *"It is easier for heaven and earth to disappear than for the least stroke of a pen to drop out of the Law"* (Luke 16:17, NIV). In addition, Jesus stated that His words would spread around the world: *"And this gospel of the kingdom will be preached in the whole world as a testimony to all nations, and then the end will come"* (Matthew 24:14, NIV). *"And the gospel must first be preached to all nations"* (Mark 13:10, NIV). What we find today is that God's Word has been preserved and has been preached throughout the world.

The Bible is the most read and studied of all historical books and remains available in many languages, more than any other book. Yet people today resist reading and studying the Bible for reasons given in the Prologue, Nature of Mankind, in the book, *World in Denial - Defiant Nature of Mankind (Prophetic Evidence for a Divine Creator)*.

Index

Adam and Eve, 16, 17-18, 22, 24, 27, 31-34, 36-41, 43-44, 60, 66, 71, 92

Angels,
    choirs of, 8-10, 22
    roles of, 10, chapter 2
    Seraphim, 8-9, 22-23
    Cherubim, 8-9, 22-23
    Guardian, 8-11

Antediluvian period, chapter 6

Children of God, 17-19, 68, 70

Death,
    physical, 34, 38-39
    spiritual, 34, 38-39, 62

Disease, 21, 26, 37, 43, 54-55, 61, 63, 71-72; see genetic burden and mutational load

Evil,
    defeating evil, chapter 8
    moral evil, 21, 43, 54-55, 61, 71-72
    physical evil, 21, 37, 43, 54-55, 57, 61, 66, 71-73
    problem with, chapter 7
    origin of, chapter 4

Flood, worldwide, 46

Free will, vii, 5, 18, 22-27, 31, 33-34, 37-38, 43, 53-63, 65, 72, 77, 81, 92-93

Free will, conflict with love and evil, 24, 27, 34, 53, 58

Garden of Eden, 16-17, 19, 32, 35, 40, 47

Genetic burden (mutational load), 6, 37, 43, 71

God's,
    answer to sin, chapter 8
    best possible solution, chapter 8
    evidence of His existence, appendix D
    limitations, 55-56
    provision for sin, chapter 8
    testing ground, chapter 8
    who is, 1-2, 13-14, 38, 68
    where is, 4, 6, 10, 26-27, 69, 80, 82, 85

Hell, appendix C

Love, vi, vii, 1, 2, 5, 7-8, 18, 22-27, 31, 33-34, 38-39, 43, 45, 53-63, 65-68, 70, 76-81

Lucifer, 8, 22-26, 28, 31, 34, 37, 55-56, 72

Mankind,
    creation of, 16, appendix D
    defiance of, 49
    fall of, chapter 5
    purpose of, 16, 18, 39, 63

Mutational Load (genetic burden), 6, 37, 43, 71

Pain and suffering, vii, 21, 26, 37, 41, 43, 54-59, 61, 63, appendix B

Pangaea (supercontinent), 14-16, 19, 46-48, 84, chapters 3 and 6

Repentance, 24, 33, 39, 61, 63, 66-70, 78-82, 87

Satan, 5, 23, 25-34, 40, 60, 65, 72, 75, 79

Separation from God, 34, 38, 43, 59, 62, 66, 71, 77, 79

Sinful act (first), chapter 4

Thermodynamics, First and Second Laws of, 2, 6, 36-37, 43, 54, 62, 71, 83, 92

Bibliography

Albright, W.F. (1956). Archaeology and the Religions of Israel. Baltimore: Johns Hopkins University Press; as cited in McDowell, J. (1972); and Albright, W.F. (1960). *The Archaeology of Palestine*. Rev. ed. Harmondsworth, Middlesex: Pelican Books; as cited in McDowell, J., op. cit.

Alcorn, R. (2009). *If God is Good.* Colorado Springs, CO: Multnomah Books.

Alcorn, R. (2013, 2017). *Seeing the Unseen*. Colorado Springs, CO: Multnomah Books.

Arnaud, M. (2017). *God and the Problem of Evil.* All About God, Purpose of Angels – What the Bible Says About Angels, 4th Para. Retrieved September 2017, from https://www.allaboutgod.com/purpose-of-angels-faq.htm.

Bates, G. Who made God? Can there be an uncreated creator? CD Produced by Creation Ministries International, www.Creation.com.

Bickel, B. and Jantz, S. (2017). *Answering the Toughest Questions about Suffering and Evil*. Bloomington, MI: Bethany House Publishers.

Boa, Kenneth (2006). How Accurate is the Bible? Retrieved 2014, from https://bible.org/article/howaccurate-bible. op. cit.

Boa, K. (2006), op. cit.

Brace, R.A. (July 12, 2011). Can Satan Still Enter Heaven to Accuse the Brethren?

Burrows, M. (1956). *What Mean These Stories?* NY: Meridian Books; as cited in McDowell, J., op. cit.

Catchpoole, D., Sarfati, J., and Wieland, C. (2008). *The Creation Answers Book*. (D. Batten, Ed.). Atlanta, GA: Creation Book Publishers.

ChurchPOP (October 2015). A Beautiful Explanation of the 9 Choirs of Angels, In One Simple Infographic. Retrieved September 2017, from https://churchpop.com/2015/10/07/a-beautiful-explanation-of-the-9-choirs-of-angels-in-one-simple-infographic/.

Collett, S., *All About the Bible.* Old Tappan: Revell, N.D.; as cited in McDowell, J., op. cit.

Cooper, David L. (1942). *The World's Greatest Library Graphically Illustrated*. Los Angeles, CA: *Biblical Research Society*; as cited in LaHaye, T. and Ice, T. (2001). *Charting the End Times*. Eugene, OR: Harvest House Publishers.

Deem, Rich (September 2007). Man, created in the image of God: How mankind is unique among all other creatures on earth. Retrieved July 2008, from http://godandscience.org/evolution/imageofgod.html.

Deffinbaugh, B, (May 2004). The Fall of Man in God's Perfect Plan. Retrieved June 2017, from https://bible.org/seriespage/5-fall-man-gods-perfect-plan.

Dillow, J.C. (1982). *The Waters Above*. Chicago, IL: Moody Press.

Gallop, R.G. (2011, 2nd. ed. 2014, revised 2016, 2018, 2021). *evolution – The Greatest Deception in Modern History*. Red Butte Press, Inc.

Gallop, R.G. (2017, revised 2019, 2021). *World in Denial - Defiant Nature of Mankind*. Red Butte Press, Inc.

Geisler, N.L. (2011). *If God, Why Evil?* Bloomington, MI: Bethany House Publishers.

Glueck, N. (1969). *Rivers in the Desert; History of Neteg.* Philadelphia: Jewish Publications Society of America; as cited in McDowell, J. (1972), op. cit.

Goldberg, D. The Fall of Man. Retrieved June 2017, from daniel@way-out-web.com.

Got Questions. How Did The Fall Affect Humanity? Got Questions.org.

Got Questions.org; Retrieved http://www.gotquestions.org/canon-Bible.html; and All About Truth. Retrieved 2014, from http://www.allabouttruth.org/bible-manuscripts-faq.htm.

Got Questions, Does God still have access to Heaven? Got Questions.org

Hagee, J. (2006). *Jerusalem Countdown: A Warning to the World.* Lake Mary, FL: FrontLine.

Ham, S. (August 15, 2015). What is the Image of God? https://answersingenesis.org/genesis/what-is-image-of-god/

Ham, K., Sarfati, J., and Wieland, C. (1990). *The Revised & Expanded Answers Book.* Green Forest, AR: Master Books. Also see Butt, Kyle (2007). The Unity of the Bible. Montgomery, AL: Apologetics Press. Retrieved 2014, from http://www.apologeticspress.org/APContent.aspx?category=13&article=2151.

Johnson, J. (November 2011). Human suffering: Why this isn't the "best of all possible worlds." *Acts & Facts*, 40 (11), Dallas, TX: Institute for Creation Research (ICR.org).

Keller, T. (2008). *The Reason for God.* New York: Dutton, 30; as cited in Alcorn, op. cit., 215.

Kenyon, F.G. (1941). *Our Bible and the Ancient Manuscripts.* New York: Harper and Brothers; as cited in McDowell, J., op. cit.

Konig, G. and Konig, R. (1984; 3rd Edition revised). *100 prophecies.* George Konig and Ray Konig. See www.100prophecies.org and McDowell, J., op. cit.

LaHaye, T. and Ice, T. (2001). *Charting the End Times.* Eugene, OR:Harvest House Publishers.

Lewis, C.S. (1952). *Mere Christianity.* NY: Harper Collins Publishers, chapters 1-4. Also see Collins, Francis S. (2006). *The Languages of God.* NY: Free Press.

Lewis, C.S. (1940). *The Problem of Pain*, New York: McMillan.

Lindsey, Hal (November 6, 2015). *The Hal Lindsey Report*, News from Hal Lindsey Media Ministry, (www.hallindsey.org). Also see http://z3news.com/w/warning-sexual-immoralityincrease-2013/.

Lindsey, Hal (March 20, 2015; March 27, 2015; September 4, 2015), op. cit.

Lindsey, Hal (December 30, 2016), *The Hal Lindsey Report*, News from Hal Lindsey Media Ministries (www.hallindsey.org).

Lindsey, Hal (February 16, 2018), *The Hal Lindsey Report*, News from Hal Lindsey Media Ministries (www.hallindsey.org).

Lockyer, Herbert, Jr. (1995). *All the Angels in the Bible*, Hendrickson Publishers Marketing, LLC, Peabody, MA. Rewrite of original work by his father, *The Mystery and Ministry of Angels*, Plymouth Rock Foundation.

McDowell, J. (1972). *Evidence that Demands a Verdict.* San Bernardino, CA: Campus Crusade for Christ.

Mitchell, T. (December 2011). Death and Steve Jobs. *Answers Update*, 18(12), Hebron, KY: Answers in Genesis. (answeresingenesis.org)

Morris, J.D. (2017). Where Was the Garden of Eden Located? Retrieved October 2017, from http://www.icr.org/article/where-was-garden-eden-located/; Morris, J.D. 1999. Where Was the Garden of Eden Located? *Acts & Facts*. 28 (12).

Morris, H.M. (1956). *The Bible and Modern Science*. Chicago: Moody Press; as cited in http://www.seeking4truth.com/historical_accuracy_of_the_bible.htm.

Morris, H.M. The scientific case against evolution. Institute for Creation Research. Retrieved October 2014, from http://www.icr.org/home/resources/resources_tracts_scientificcaseagainstevolution/.

NIV Study Bible (1985), Passage taken from the introduction to the Book of Amos, New International Version, Zondervan Publishing House, Grand Rapids, MI 49506.

Pratte, D.E. (1988, 2000). God Desires All Men to Know, Believe & Obey His Will; as cited in http://www.gospelway.com/bible/bible_preservation.php.

Ramm, B. (1957). *Protestant Christian Evidences*. Chicago: Moody Press; as cited in McDowell, J., op. cit. and Boa, K. (2006), op. cit.

Ramm, B. (1957), op. cit.; as cited in McDowell; and Matthews, M. (May 25, 2014). The Preservation of the Bible. *Answers in Genesis;* retrieved from https://answersingenesis.org/the-word-of-god/the-preservation-of-the-bible/.

Reardon, J. (2013). What does it mean to fear God? *Christianity Today International;* Retrieved July 2016, from http://www.christianitytoday.com/biblestudies/bible-answers/spirituallife/what-does-it-mean-to-fear-god.html.

Russell, E. Angels and the Hierarchy of the Heavenlies. *Blaze Magazine Online*. Retrieved June 2017, from http://www.flamcministries.org/angels.htm.

Sasser, J. (2003). The Historical Accuracy of the Bible. La Vista Church of Christ. Retrieved 2014, from http://www.lavistachurchofchrist.org/LVarticles/HistoricalAccuracyOfTheBible.htm.

Scroggie, W. Graham (1953). *The Unfolding Drama of Redemption*. London: Pickering & Inglis Ltd. Also cited in Whitcomb, J.C., and Morris, H.M. (1961). *The Genesis Flood*. Phillipsburg, NJ: The Presbyterian and Reformed Publishing Company.

Smith, W. (1961). *The Incomparable Book*. Beacon Publications; as cited in McDowell, J.

Stedman, Ray C. (1978). The Tower of Babel. Retrieved April 2008, from http://www.idolphin.org/babel.html (adapted from Stedman, Ray C. (1978). *The Beginnings*. Waco Books). Also see http://www.raystedman.org/genesis/.

Thaxton, C.B., Bradley, W.L., and Olsen, R.L. (1984). *The Mystery of Life's Origin*. Dallas, TX: Lewis and Stanley; as cited in Catchpoole, D., Sarfati, J., and Wieland, C. (2008). *The Creation Answers Book*. (D. Batten, Ed.). Atlanta, GA: Creation Book Publishers.

Wallace, J.W., What does it mean to have been created in the "image of God"? https://coldcasechristianity.com/writings/what-does-it-mean-to-have-been-created-in-the-image-of-god/

Whitcomb, J.C. (1988). *The World That Perished*. Grand Rapids, MI: Baker Book House.

Wilson, R.D. (1959). *A Scientific Investigation of the Old Testament*. Chicago: Moody Press; as cited in McDowell, J., op. cit.

www.ingramcontent.com/pod-product-compliance
Lightning Source LLC
Chambersburg PA
CBHW080924170426
43201CB00016B/2257